Performance Marketing for Professionals

An Introduction to Performance Marketing

By: Murray Newlands
&
John Rampton

Performance Marketing for Professionals

DEDICATION

You the reader and our best wishes for your success!

Disclaimer & Terms of Use Agreement

The authors and publisher of this e-book have used their best efforts in preparing the accompanying materials. The authors and publisher make no representation or warranties with respect to the accuracy, applicability, fitness, or completeness of the contents of this e-book. The information contained in this e-book is strictly for educational purposes. Therefore, if you wish to apply ideas contained in this e-book, you are taking full responsibility for your actions.

The authors and publisher disclaim any warranties (express or implied), merchantability, or fitness for any particular purpose. The authors and publisher shall in no event be held liable to any party for any direct, indirect, punitive, special, incidental or other consequential damages arising directly or indirectly from any use of this material, which is provided "as is", and without warranties. As always, the advice of a competent legal, tax, accounting or other professional should be sought. The authors and publisher do not warrant the performance, effectiveness or applicability of any sites listed or linked to in this e-book. All links are for information purposes only and are not warranted for content, accuracy or any other implied or explicit purpose.

Murray Newlands

Murray Newlands is the founder and editor of The Mail www.themail.com and editor of the Money Maker Discussion blog. He founded The Mail in 2013 where he writes and makes videos about performance marketing covering topics as broad as email marketing, lead generation, mobile marketing as well as content marketing. Murray is an advisor to a number of bay area startups including VigLink. In 2011 Wiley published his book <u>Online Marketing: A User's Manual.</u> Born in England Murray moved to the USA in 2011 being recognized by the US government as an alien of extraordinary ability. Murray is a winner of the prestigious AFFY award.

John Rampton

John Rampton is an entrepreneur, online marketing guru, and startup addict. He's written for many major publications such as the Huffington Post, Entrepreneur, Examiner, Search Engine Journal, and Bing. He's the Founder of www.Artscience.com

John has spoken at BlogWorld, Affiliate Summit, SES, and several other conferences. He has been written about on Forbes as being a leading blogging expert. He made Hanapin Marketing's "Top 25 Most Influential PPC Experts" in the world for 2012. He was number 10 on the list.

Chapter 1:

Introduction

This book is a top to bottom guide to affiliate marketing. If you are new to affiliate marketing and want to know what it is, whether or not your company should be doing it, or how to be an affiliate, then this book is for you.

What Is Affiliate Marketing?

Affiliate marketing, also known as performance marketing, is a digital marketing practice where an "affiliate," normally the owner of a website, sends traffic to another website—"the advertiser"—and does so for a reward. The reward is normally paid as a success fee when the traffic sent by the affiliate completes a purchase or fills in an enquiry form from the advertiser.

A good example of this would be a book club organizer telling their club members that they will be reading a particular book and that the book could be bought on Amazon. As part of Amazon's affiliate program, the owner of the book club would be supplied with a specific "affiliate" link from Amazon, which he would share with the members of his club. When members click on the link or banner from the organizer and purchase the book on Amazon, Amazon would track those sales and reward the book club owner for the sales by paying them a percentage of the sale value, say 5%.

This traditional model of affiliate marketing has been extended around the world and has come to incorporate many different models such as paying for clicks, leads, page views, downloads, and more.

What Is An Affiliate?

An affiliate, sometimes known as a publisher or performance marketer, is a person or company that drives traffic to another person or company for a reward. Traditionally, an affiliate was the owner of a website such as a blog or forum, but now, an affiliate could be someone who develops and manages apps for your smartphone or tablet. Many affiliate work without owning their own traffic sources—one example being media buying. If an affiliate knows what the advertiser will pay for traffic, or for a person who buys an item, then they can buy adverts on Facebook or Google to drive traffic that make purchases. If the cost of buying that traffic is less than the amount that they get paid by the advertiser as a reward, then the affiliate will make a profit.

Affiliates used to be predominantly small companies run by one person, but as affiliate marketing has grown, so has the shape and nature of affiliates. There are large affiliate companies with hundreds of customers, and there are even TV stations that will run advertisements on a performance basis.

What Is An Advertiser?

An advertiser, sometimes called a merchant, can be any kind of business that wants to gain more customers and is willing to pay affiliates on a reward basis. Traditionally, advertisers were companies that sold things online, however, there are now tens of thousands of companies using affiliate marketing to promote themselves around the world. With the proliferation of online advertisers, the nature of what they are willing to pay for has changed, too. Initially, advertisers paid on a cost per sale model, but as the need to speak to customers on the phone grew, lots of companies began to pay for customers who fill in a form (lead generation) or call them on the phone (cost per call). As potential customers continue to use their smartphones to access the Internet more and more, cost per call campaigns have become more popular.

What Is An Affiliate Network?

Affiliate networks provide the tracking software to advertisers and affiliates to enable them to track and report the transactions that affiliates get paid for. Affiliate networks also provide one point of payment for advertisers and use that money to pay hundreds or hundreds of thousand of affiliates.

There are many advantages for an advertiser to use an affiliate network. First of all, the advertiser does not need to create their own software solution; they can use one that is provided by the network. Paying lots of individual affiliates can be time consuming, and affiliate networks can work the advertiser to make sure that they have their program setup correctly in the first place to ensure that it's successful. Affiliate networks have expertise in reaching and working with affiliates to get the most traffic and sales possible for the advertiser. Networks can also be experts in detecting fraud.

The disadvantage to the advertiser is that the network charges a fee, typically between 10 and 30% of the revenue paid to affiliates, as well as a monthly fee for providing this service. There is a potential lack of communication between the advertiser and the affiliates.

There are also many advantages for affiliates that work with networks. An affiliate can promote many different advertisers, but registering with each advertiser, managing those relationships, and billing each of them individually could be very time consuming. Affiliate networks provide a one-stop shop for affiliates to login and work with any number of different advertisers. In theory, affiliate networks provide an independent tracking system to ensure that the affiliate gets paid for all their work, and since the network is paid a percentage of the sales, it's in their interest to track as many as possible. Furthermore, networks can provide information, advice, and additional services to affiliates that advertisers would not have the experience to provide.

The disadvantage for affiliates is that networks take a percentage of their sales. Because of this, some affiliates prefer to work directly with advertisers so that they can earn more money. This option is normally only available to large affiliates.

Advertisers Running In-House Programs

Advertisers can chose to run their own affiliate programs, too. They can develop their own tracking software, or choose to use a pre-existing software solution to manage their tracking. While this is not an exclusive or exhaustive list, some popular solutions include Hasoffers, GetCake, LinkTrust, Impacket

Raduius, PHG.

Who Runs Affiliate Programs?

Amazon, eBay, Barnes & Noble, American Airlines, Macy's, Disney, Sony, Netflix, 1800 Flowers, and the list goes on. Lots of smaller local companies run affiliate programs, too.

Chapter 2

The Sales Funnel

What Is The Sales Funnel and Where You Want To Be On The Sales Cycle?

The Basic Overview

The sales funnel is a metaphor that is used to describe the sales process from the perspective of the buyer. Think of it as a process with a wide top with lots of people, and a narrow bottom with only a few people. Here's an example for how that might look.

A lot of people enjoy gardening, and often wonder how to properly maintain a lush and thriving garden of their own, however, the number of people that actively seek out and purchase books on how to do so is much smaller.

1. People start out thinking that they need to find out about how to look after their garden.

2. They search online and discover that they can buy a book that will teach them how to look after their garden.

3. They decide that they want to buy a book about how to look after their garden.

4. They look for a book about how to look after their garden.

5. They look for a book about their specific kind of garden; one with clay soil in New England, for example.

6. They read reviews of the few books available about looking after gardens in New England.

7. They decide on the book that they want to buy, and then search for the cheapest place possible to buy that book.

8. They look for a discount code for that book.

9. They buy the book.

Smaller Numbers

At each stage of the sales funnel there are less and less people searching for products or services. The closer you are to the bottom of the sales funnel, the more likely the person is to buy the book. In the traditional affiliate model, the last person's tracking to record a consumer's action is the person to get paid.

Higher Value Lower Down The Funnel

The further down the funnel the consumer is, the more valuable they are to an affiliate. Someone who is looking for books on gardening is much less valuable than someone who is looking for the cheapest place to buy a specific book. The person looking for a discount code is often already on the checkout page and ready to submit their credit card in another browser window. This is one reason why making discount code and coupon sites have been very popular with affiliates.

Attribution

Some advertisers have started to realize that rewarding affiliates along the way can increase brand awareness and overall sales volumes. As an alternative to last touch counting, some affiliate programs now share the reward among various pieces of the sales funnel.

Attribution and What To Look For

By: Adam Riemer

Attribution is one of the most important things you can look at when evaluating the value of an affiliate, or your program. By setting up a cross channel attribution model and properly crediting the right channel you can know where to spend your budget, which partners or channels are working to funnel off sales and cost you more money, as well as which affiliate partners you should remove from your program. The time the cookie is set on your timeline is a huge indicator to who is adding value and who is not.

If the cookie is dropped while the person is on your site, it could be a toolbar, PPV, or other forms of adware. If it's set on your site during the closing of the sale, the sale could have been poached by a person looking for a coupon code and the coupon site, or adware taking credit for a sale that they didn't add value to. They just showed a coupon when the person typed in your URL or trademark + coupons into a search engine. By ranking your own sites for these terms or not allowing affiliates to rank for them organically or with PPC, you can properly allocate the money lost to channels that are adding more value or invest in affiliates that send new customers and help actually convert visitors to sales.

One other scenario is the review site when someone is actually comparison-shopping. You can see where they came from, if they shopped through comparison engines and review sites, and also see whether the positive, negative, and mixed reviews helped to close a sale. This is different than the coupon site or trademark bidder that ranks for your terms, because this actually helped close a sale, not just set a cookie by providing something you could do on your own in the last minute.

Attribution is one of the best indicators of a profitable program. Affiliates should know where they add value or where they take away, and merchants need to learn how to look at proper attribution. It will help you keep your budget focused on the most profitable channels, let you know which affiliates you should keep, which you should remove, and which you may want to give increased or decreased commissions to.

How Can You Use This?

If you are going to make a content site about a topic, think about making content for the bottom of the funnel. Include product reviews and information about where and how to buy products and services—buyer's guides are always a popular option. Think about how you can draw people down the sales funnel. Have a buyer's guide with lots of pages of content at the top of the funnel, and then link at the bottom of the page to the buyer's guide so you get the most traffic in, but you draw them down the funnel on your site and get them maximum value out of them. You can do this with traffic from search engines, Email, or PPC.

Conclusion

The sales funnel is a metaphor for describing the part of the sales process people are in. There is more traffic available— and it's normally cheaper—if you are buying traffic for people who are at the top of the sales funnel. People who are at the bottom of the sales funnel are more valuable for affiliates and advertisers because they are more likely to buy products.

Chapter 3:

Choosing What To Promote

Everyone has their own strategies for choosing what to promote and a lot of the decisions will be based on the kind of traffic you have. Here are some alternative methods:

Chose What You Know.

If you are going to promote something, it helps if you know the product well and understand the consumer and their motivations for purchasing it. If you are a sports fan, for example, you understand why people buy sports memorabilia, and will probably know that sports fans are much more likely to buy team memorabilia after winning a big game or a championship than at other times during the season. Also, the longer you promote something, the more you come to understand it, the more contact you have, and the better the commissions become, which ultimately puts you in a better place to make more money from the traffic you have.

If you are going to make content sites, and also produce content for other sites with links back to yours, then you should choose a topic that you love. You better be passionate about the content because in order to be successful, you will have to write a lot about it and create informative, valuable, and consistent content. People are more likely to succeed in the long term with content sites about something they care about, talk about, and have friends in common to talk about related topics. One of the common killers of affiliate projects is that people simply become bored with a content site.

Tips For Content Site Makers

1. Google AdWords and other dynamic adserving platforms are a good place to start when making a content site. If you don't know what advertisements are going to work well, try Google AdWords. These self optimize, showing the most relevant ads to your content. While this might not be the highest revenue source, it is certainly a good start.

2. Once you have run Google AdWords for a short time, try looking at the advertisements appearing on your site and see if they have affiliate programs. Test out those programs and see if you get a better result. You should also look at their competitors and give them a try.

3. Review your competitors and see what advertisements they are running, as well as what they are writing about. Pay particularly close attention to the content about company products and services. This will give you a good source of potential affiliate programs.

4. Expand the search for what to promote on your content site. If you are a larger affiliate, Linkdex has a tool that can show the affiliate links to a program. By searching the links for the programs you're running, you'll be able to find new sites that you're competing with and what programs they're running.

Ask Your Affiliate Manager

When you sign up with an affiliate network you will be given an affiliate manager. Every network normally has some top performing affiliate offers that are hot at that time—the 80%/20% rule. They should be able to tell you a number of offers that are performing well with what you want to do and should be able to help you. However, a word of warning:

affiliate managers are sometimes pressured by their network managers to promote less popular campaigns that are not as effective, so be aware of that.

League Tables

Affiliate networks, as well as some of the offer directories publish their data in such as way as to enable you to see what are the best performing offers in any one sector.

Facebook Ad Buying

Open Facebook; see what everyone else is running and do it better. If you spot someone else running a campaign on Facebook, you may be able to make a better ad, run better targeting, or have a better converting landing page.

Affiliates have been known to setup various Facebook profiles with different ages, genders, and interest information and see what adverts show up. This will show you what other people are advertising to these types of consumers and will give you ideas about what affiliate offers you could promote to them. Warning: setting up multiple fake profiles is against the Facebook terms of service and may be illegal where you are.

Email Affiliates

If you are running a newsletter, you can also drive traffic as an affiliate. The trick is to setup emails in Gmail, look at what's coming into your inbox and what offers you are receiving. Remember to check your spam folder, as some of their affiliate offers may land there.

More Tips for Choosing Which Offer to Run:

Seasonality

At times like Christmas, Valentines Day, Mothers Day, and other holidays, different types of offers may outperform each other.

Just before the end of the month, short-term loan offers can do well.

In January, with New Year's resolutions, health club, diet, and dating offers do well.

If you are in the travel industry, you know that there are different seasons for booking sky holidays and summer holidays.

Look out for big events—the Olympics are very tight on some affiliate offers, but beer sales and barbeque sales usually perform very well.

A bad flu season will result in an increased demand for orange juice.

Sports betting is big during the Super Bowl.

Follow the news and Google trends for update and opportunities

Competition

Competition can be good and bad.

The best offers are often widely promoted in the market place. Netflix is a very popular service and if it converts well, it will be a great offer in the marketplace if you have a movie website. On the flipside, trying to make your site rank for "buy Netflix" is going to be super competitive. Sometime choosing offers that are less competitive can be more productive and valuable then going for the hot offer of the moment.

Long-Term Offers or Short-Term Trends

If you can spot a trend and present a great offer, you can make a lot of money fast. If you are new to affiliate marketing and are trying to work things out, it can be difficult to learn as the market changes and you are testing things at a fast pace. Choose an offer based on your experience and whether or not you can make it work. If you notice a trend, but don't know how to make it convert, you're better off leaving it along and seeking out a different offer.

Traffic Converts Differently From Different Sources

I have run offers via Email that converted well, but those same offers ended up converting horribly from content-based traffic. If you are running different types of traffic, expect offers to perform differently.

Offers Come And Go

Advertisers come and go, and what's hot at one time may not be hot later. Markets change over time and consumer needs change. Make sure you know what the best deal is at the time and follow what is happening in the market. Blockbuster video was once a hot brand that consumers loved, and now it's irrelevant because very few people even have video players any more. Advertisers that want to grow will sometimes pay above market rate to acquire new customers and affiliates can cash in.

Conclusion

Spend time to research the best deals for your traffic and research what everyone else is doing. It may take you some time to work out the best deals for your traffic sources, but in the long run, developing and utilizing a well-informed strategy will make you the most money.

Chapter 4:

Registering With Affiliate Networks and Getting Approved

What Networks Want

Affiliate Networks work hard to get good advertisers and they want to keep them, along with high quality traffic that converts well and delivers good volume.

Affiliate managers are tasked with finding good affiliates and working with them to get lots of high quality traffic and make a lot of sales for their advertisers. They have specific goals for each advertiser, and they will push you to meet their targets.

Networks and affiliate managers are afraid of affiliates who might lose them time, money, and advertisers, and they're wary of affiliate fraud.

A bad scenario for an affiliate manager is a new affiliate, often from a foreign country, that uses fraudulent technology to drive face sales or leads that they pay money to. The advertiser does not accept the sales or leads and complains, does not pay, or leaves the network. In turn, the network loses the opportunity to make money with that advertiser and loses the money that they have paid out. Furthermore, the network will get a bad reputation in the industry and advertisers refuse to work with them.

Networks Want Affiliates That Send Good Traffic to Their Advertisers

Many of the very best advertisers and the best campaigns are not available to most affiliates. The large affiliate networks and advertisers keep them hidden because they're afraid of fraudulent affiliates, and they like to reward their best affiliates with great opportunities.

How Can You Become the Type of Affiliate That Networks and Affiliate Managers Want to Work With?

Make it obvious to them that you are a real person. That includes being on Facebook, going to affiliate events, and meeting them in person. Be available to talk with them via Email and on the phone. If they want to talk with you on Skype, show your face. They will want to know how you are driving traffic to their advertisers. You don't need to show them everything, but you will want to be able to show them enough. You might want to setup a website about you and your affiliate work. Affiliate managers use Google to search people too!

Most good affiliate networks and affiliate managers will want to talk to you on the phone before they approve you to run their campaigns. Prepare what you're going to tell them before they call. There's no shame in saying you're new to affiliate marketing, but be ready to explain how you are going to promote their offers.

If you find an offer that you want to run, and it's on multiple networks, you could apply to multiple affiliate networks at the same time. Some networks are faster than others at approving affiliates.

Pick Up The Phone

If you're waiting to be approved by a network, pick up the phone, call the network, and ask to be approved. Most affiliates are too lazy to do this and it will push you to the front of the line.

Where Are You From?

It is true that you are more likely to be approved for an affiliate program if you live in the same country as the affiliate network or rep that you're dealing with. Many affiliate programs are on multiple networks and some of those networks may have an affiliate representative in your country, so try and find them.

Introductions Count

Just like most things in life, if you can find an affiliate who has a relationship with a network or an affiliate manager who can introduce you to the contact; that will greatly improve your chances of getting accepted.

What If You Get Rejected?

If you get rejected, ask the network why you have been rejected. Affiliate networks and manages have to approve thousands of affiliates and it's often pushed to the most junior person to make judgment calls about your credibility. Most scammers never phone networks and would never ask why they were rejected. Calling the network and asking will force someone to take another look at your application. Most scammers would never do this, so it makes you look much more credible. Normally, someone with more seniority will review rejected affiliates who ask for a review, so you will probably get someone much more skilled to review your application if you call. You have nothing to lose by asking them to review the rejection; it could just be someone clicked the wrong button!

Getting The Best Deal

Once you have narrowed down what you're going to promote, start to do your research on how to get the best deal. Many advertisers are listed on a number of networks. Research what the best deal is for you and make sure you are getting the most money from your traffic.

Look at sites like OfferVault that will show you which networks individual advertisers are listed on, as well as the payouts.

Asking For A Higher Payout

Do not be afraid to ask your affiliate manager for a higher payout, they can only say no. If you are going to ask for a higher payout, be prepared to say why you should get a higher payout.

If another network has the same advertiser with a higher payout ask the affiliate manger for that higher rate. Do not take their word that you are getting the best payout available in the market—they might not know that someone has the same offer available for a higher payout.

If you think you can drive more traffic, then that's a good reason for asking for a higher payout.

Once You Get Accepted, Build A Reputation With Your Representative

Getting to know your affiliate manager matters. They can offer help and advice, and may be able to increase payouts and speed up payments. Affiliate managers may also have short-term campaigns with high payouts, as well as exclusive campaigns that are not available to all affiliates. They can also act as a reference to other affiliate managers; so, getting to know your affiliate manager can be extremely advantageous.

If you are new and are lucky enough to drive a lot of traffic, your affiliate manager may become suspicious if you're not in contact with them—that's what fraudulent affiliates do. They sign up to new affiliate offers, send lots of traffic, take the money, and hope to vanish before anyone really knows whom they are. It's in your best interest as an affiliate to avoid behavior like this.

Chapter 5:

Link Management

If you are going to be setting up lots of affiliate links, you should think about how you are going to manage that process from the start.

There are a number to third party tools that you can use to help with this process. Tools commonly used for managing links include Tracking 202/Prosper 202, bevomedia, niftystats, and link tracker.

Why Would You Want To Use Third Party Tools To Manage Your Links?

Let's say, for example, that you are testing out running multiple campaigns and buying traffic on Google, Bing and Facebook.

Looking at one of these software tools as an example, Tracking 202 offers the following:

One reporting system to track, monitor, and calculate all your PPC accounts and campaigns

"EPC Calculator

T202 maximizes EPC (Earnings Per Click) calculations. How would you feel if you knew exactly what you needed to bid for a keyword for it to be profitable? Then you could adjust your bids accordingly and turn a profit within seconds.

Know your EPC:

- EPC per Keyword
- EPC per Text Ad

- EPC per Referrer
- EPC per PPC Account

Spy View

Spy view is a feature you will only find on T202. With Spy View, you can see real-time actions your visitors make with your ads. What's more, you can subscribe to your own Spy View RSS feeds to get up-to-the-second information anywhere!

Top-Performing Keywords

T202 tells you which keywords are making you money and which ones are losing you money. So you can weed out the losers and turn any campaign into a profit monster!

Keyword Cloaking

T202 gives users the ability to cloak their keywords from advertisers and affiliate networks-so all of your top-performing keywords are a secret.

Why risk your Affiliate Manager or the Advertiser finding out your best keywords, copying them for their own campaigns, and putting you out of business?

To be successful at Affiliate Marketing you must track your keywords and they must be cloaked.

Direct Linking a Landing Pages

T202 works with direct linking through PPC campaigns or with your own landing pages. Now you can track whether your campaigns profit more with direct linking or landing pages."

They also offer a free, self-hosted version called Prosper 202 if you don't want anyone else to be able to see your data.

Link Checking

If you are serious about being an affiliate, you might want to consider using a link checker. Not everyone sees these as necessary, and some people are very happy to visually check all their links.

Once you have your links set up and working you need to make sure that they continue to work. Believe it or not, advertisers change their sales pages without telling their affiliates. There is nothing more annoying than driving traffic to an advertiser who has changed or removed their sales page.

One of the tools that does this is called "Offer Snitch." It automatically checks the sales pages of the offers you're running and sends you an alert if they change.

Chapter 6:

Email Marketing

Send Consumers What They Want

When people ask about making money with Email marketing, I have one simple answer, which is, send people what they want to receive. You should know where they opted in and what they opted in for, so be sure to send them related things that they will like, click on, and sign up to use or purchase. If someone registers for a competition to win a vacation on your site, then send them more information about other people's competitions to win a vacation. If they registered for a loan application, send them more finance related offers. If you blindly send irrelevant offers then there's no value in your Emails. If you send good quality content in the form of a deal or a newsletter, customers may even send it on and help grow your list.

List Development

If you're going to get started Email marketing as an affiliate, the best way to do it is to grow your own list. If you have a site with lots of traffic, you can ask the visitors to subscribe.

Putting up an Email subscription box is the best way of doing this. Many sites use "pop up boxes" to encourage people to subscribe. Sometimes this covers up the page to make the user subscribe before they see the content. A cookie is then placed on the user's computer so that they do not see the pop up box again. You might want to look at services such as Pop Up Domination to help with this.

Many sites provide further incentives to encourage subscription. Some of the common things offered to encourage subscription include unique content that's available only to subscribers such as a white paper, an E-book, or entry to a competition.

Co-Registration

Co-registration is probably something you have seen, but not necessarily realized what was going on when you saw it. When someone signs up to your email newsletter you can offer them the opportunity to register to other email newsletters at the same time—this is co-registration. As people register for your newsletter, other newsletter list owners can pay you for these co-registrations. You can also buy these registrations on other people's Email newsletter opt-ins to grow your list, or you can trade newsletter registrants—we recommend trying regready.com for this.

Buying/Sharing Data Versus Growing Your Own List

You might be great at generating an Email list, but no good at making money from them. The good news is that there's an entire industry that focuses on working with others to monetize the data that you generate. If you're not good at generating Email data but are great at creating offers, writing newsletters, or just getting people to open and click on your emails, then you can work with other people to help make money by using their data. If you need data to monetize, the best people to work with are people that you know and people that are collecting data that is similar to yours. There are companies that broker data between list owners such as Right 1 Data and Digital Bulldogs.

Cleaning Your Data

When you are collecting data, think about the quality of the data that you're collecting and the reasons why people may give you fake information. If you're collecting lots of data and people are giving you fake information, or you're managing someone else's data, you might think about getting your data cleaned—promoting offers to a bad list is a waste of your time and money. Trying to send Emails to spam traps or addresses that don't exist will reduce your deliverability and can get your IP's banned. There are companies that make a living suing people who send them spam.

Sending Names

The audience you're sending Emails to will look at the "from" address. Use the name of your website, or, if you're sending out from a personal account, think about an appropriate name. If you're sending in the US, you might want to use a typical American name as the "from" name.

Subject Lines

The subject line of an Email is very important—it's the first thing you see when you open your Email inbox. The easiest way to see what works is to look at your own inbox and take note of what grabs your attention. Many offers will actually provide a subject line to go with the Email offer.

Choosing Offers

You have to obey the legal rules of the country you are sending to, but in addition to that, remember that your recipients probably already receive too many Emails. Everyone hates getting unwanted Email, so the trick is to send people mail that they want to get and will enjoy. A good place to start is to send your recipients offers that are similar to what they opted in for. When someone gets an Email, it's more of an impulse to click on it and take action. Unless you have a list of customers who have bought a specific product, sending offers in which users fill out a lead form or try a product seem to work better than asking them to simply buy a product with their credit card. At Christmas and special occasions such as Valentines Day you may see changes in that, but that's the experience that I've had and seems to be the collective wisdom of most email marketers. But try what works best for your list. Don't forget to subscribe to your competitors and see what they send you as well.

If you can segment your list, you will improve your ability to send people Email offers that they want and ultimately increase your revenue. However, you might want to take into account the time cost of segmenting your list against the perceived increased monetization.

Permission

Not all affiliate offers allow you to promote via Email. Many require you to use specific subject lines and creative. If you are going to change these things, you many need to get permission in advance.

Email Offer Cycle and Time of Day

You will want to think about the cycle of Emails that your users get as well as when they get them. I have met people whose full time job is to optimize this process. When someone registers for something, do you send them a thank you Email or a follow up Email? The top email marketers have a whole sequence of follow up Emails that continue from the registration. They may also change the pattern of follow up Emails depending on which emails those recipients open and click on.

You probably do not want to send the same offer to the same person within two weeks. It might be possible to do this if you have noticeably different creative, or a different offer from the same advertiser.

All lists perform differently. Most people send emails in the morning and get most of their opens on the first and second days of the Email send. Most lists get very poor open rates during the weekend, as people are away from their desks at work. Given this, Friday, Saturday, and Sunday are not the best days for sending emails. If you have a list of weekend activity enthusiasts, your statistics may be different.

Deliverability and Getting Into the inbox

When you start to send Emails, it's best practice to setup a number of addresses in the different domains (Hotmail, Gmail, etc.) that you're trying to send to. Make sure to send test Emails to those domains to ensure that your Emails are being delivered to the inbox. Many domains automatically look for terms commonly found in spam and automatically filter them into the spam box or bounce the message. Be careful when using terms such as "free" or "offer," as these are more likely to be filtered. Many Email platforms have a scoring system that will give you an indication of whether or not this is likely to happen.

Split Testing

Before you send the Email to your whole list, you may want to try sending different subject lines and different content to small parts of your list to see what your recipients respond to best.

Call To Action

Include a call to action, a link, or a phone number. It sounds obvious, but some people forget to ask the recipient to take the next step and respond to the offer.

Sending Your Emails and Working With an ESP

If you have data and you know what offers you want to send, you need to think about how you're going to send them to your list. Using an Email Service Provider (ESP) can be a good way to start. Not all ESP's like to work with affiliates, and some will close down your account if you try to send affiliate offers. We recommend trying www.eloop.com.

Using Hosting and an MTA

If you want to send your own Emails and have your own hosting, you can use a Mail Transfer Agent (MTA). Once you start sending lots of Emails—I mean a few million per month—you might want to setup your own hosting and your own mailing software. Expect this to run you a few thousand dollars per month, something you will only want to look at if you're doing very well. For this type of service, we recommend looking at VOLOPM and Port 25.

Buying Domain Names

Do not use GoDaddy. Not all domain registration companies like working with Email affiliates and some are very quick to block and take away domains from Email affiliates. GoDaddy has a reputation for being very quick to take away affiliate domain names. It's best to use domain names that are a few months old to send Emails.

Sending Domain Name

If you're going to start sending a large amount of Email to your subscribers, use a different domain name other than the main domain name of the site. The domain name you use to send Email can have its reputation damaged if too many people complain that Email is spam.

Most affiliate networks allow you to send Emails containing tracking links that ultimately redirect through their software, however, the domain and IP address of their tracking links are shared by their entire affiliate base. This poses a big problem when the domain gets black listed by spam monitoring services. As soon as the domain and IP addresses are black listed, it will adversely affect your ability to get Emails into inboxes. Indeed, one bad apple can spoil the whole bunch.

However, affiliate networks and advertisers utilizing LinkTrust affiliate tracking software have access to a patented solution that solves this problem. LinkTrust's "Remote Traffic Agent" issues affiliate-specific domains and IP addresses for tracking links specifically intended for Emails. In addition, new and additional domains and IP addresses can be distributed very quickly. This means your traffic is siloed from the ill effects of other affiliates and that your hard work doesn't go down the drain. Without your own assigned domain and IP address and the ability to spin up new ones incredibly fast, you could be sending quality Emails with little or no results.

IP Addresses

When you start to send Emails to Internet Service Providers (ISPs) like Hotmail and Gmail, it will take time before you're able to send a lot of Email from a new IP address. These services do reputation scoring for IP addresses and it takes them a time to trust a new IP address.

Legal

You need to know what laws apply for Email marketing in each individual country. In the USA, the CAN SPAM laws apply.

Unsubscribe Links

Make it easy and clear for people to unsubscribe. Sending people Email that they don't want will not help you generate leads or sales and will increase the chances of recipients complaining.

Suppression Lists

In the US, people opt out of receiving information that promotes a specific advertiser. Each advertiser needs to keep an up to date list of everyone who has opted out. Before you start promoting an advertiser you need to make sure that your list of Email addresses does not include anyone who has opted out of receiving promotions from that advertiser.

What Mobile Means For Email

Depending on your list, many of your Email recipients may be receiving and reading their messages on a mobile phone. At the time of writing, one affiliate told me this was up to 46% and rising. Look at the Emails that you get on your phone and find out what works best for you and what you click on. One affiliate marketing specialist told me that the time they sent the Emails to recipients who regularly opened their emails on phones was different from desktop users, they got a better open rate on Tuesday nights because people were no longer at work. The use of phones may encourage people to prefer text only emails with short URL list that is easy to click on. Filling in a long form on your phone is hard, so it may also encourage promoting offers with shorter lead generation forms. If you can pre-fill the form with data from the Email that may also help the offer convert better.

Conclusion

Email marketing can be very profitable but with more and more Emails being sent, it's becoming much more competitive. Getting past spam filters and into the inbox is getting harder all the time. People are less likely to open and respond to Emails as well. Having said that, everyone has Email and responds to some of it. Think about what Email you get and like to respond to, and how you can use that knowledge to get people to respond to your emails and make money.

Chapter 7:

Building Content Sites

Making Sites With Great Content

Making sites with great content can be a great way of promoting affiliate offers. Think about what you know and what people might be looking for when they're looking for products to purchase.

Choosing a Content Sites Subject Matter

Making a content site that gets traffic takes a lot of time and effort, so think carefully about the kind of site you're going to make and how you are going to get traffic.

Think about where your traffic is coming from and whether your site is searchable, in which case, you probably want to look at Google since it has the largest market share. It's possible that most of your traffic is going to come from social sites like Facebook.

Think about what people are going to be looking for at the bottom of the sales funnel and how you're going to convert that into sales.

Search engines prefer sites that have been around for a while, so don't expect your new site to get loads of traffic from the get-go. Also, keep in mind that this is going to be a site that you'll be working on for a while, so it helps to be passionate and knowledgeable on the subject matter. One good way to find a topic that you're interested in is trying to produce 10 pages of content about it and see if you still have more informative and valuable information to share at that point.

Managing a large number of different sites can be hard. Start with one or two sites and work with them before launching any more websites. I personally have quite a few websites that have just fallen by the wayside simply because I have lost interest in them.

Audience and Keyword Research

Google Keyword Tool is one of the best tools for finding new content ideas. It will tell you phrases that people search for, the amount of times that those phrases are being searched, and how competitive they are on PPC. Normally, words that are more competitive on PPC are more costly because they are more valuable to advertisers and to you as an affiliate.

Google predictive search is also a great way to find topics for affiliate sites. Just go to Google and start to type the phrase that you think people will search for and Google will show you the rest. These are popular searches and will give you ideas as to what people are looking for.

Twitter search and other social media searches are great places to look for ideas for affiliate sites. People often talk about things that they might not be searching for, but could be great if you can get good social media take up for your site.

Competitive market research with tools like follow.net enable you to look at other affiliate sites and see what traffic they're getting and where it's coming from. They also enable you to look at advertisers sites and see where they're getting traffic.

Domain Names

Buying the right domain name can make all the difference in the world. If you see a link and know what the site is about, then you will be more likely to click on it. For example, we all know what cheaphotels.com is about.

Making Money From Redirect Traffic

By: Scott Richter, Affiliate.com, Redirect.com

If you own domains that are generating traffic and you aren't monetizing those sites, you should look into redirect solutions. Moreover, if you own sites that are only monetizing with US ads, or you simply own a lot of domains with nothing on them, then selling that redirect traffic can be an easy source of additional revenue for you.

Many website owners only think about making money in the country that they live in or are targeting. For example, if they live in the US and run a site that's targeted towards Americans, then they will put up ads for those people and show those same ads to everyone that comes, regardless of whether or not those visitors can actually purchase the products. If someone from Sweden visits your site, you should show them Swedish ads or redirect them to a Swedish offer in order to optimize your traffic and maximize your revenue.

While buying the right domain name can play a huge role in the success of a website, there are also ways to make money from simply owning a number of domains. The technical term for this is "domaining," and it's a practice wherein users purchase numerous domains and horde them for later use, or to sell for profit. However, in order to make money from the domains you own (and not waste money collecting them), you must either set up a content site and run your own ads, or utilize a domain parking service to help you monetize your unused domains. The alternative is to simply redirect that traffic.

This is a quick, easy way to instantly monetize all of your unused traffic and domains with almost zero effort.

WordPress

Many affiliates like using WordPress to make a blog for promoting offers because it enables users to create a simple and easy-to-use website. There are lots of templates for WordPress to give your site its own customized look and feel. There are also a lot of freelancers who know how to make changes to a WordPress site, which affords a lot of support options. If you're going to make money from your website, we recommend creating your own Wordpress site.

SEO Tips

Create pages of content about the things that people are looking for and will be compelled to share on social media. Use terms that people actively search for on either search engines or social media as the page titles.

Page Names and Titles

Use descriptive words that you want to rank for at the start of the URL. Do not make these too long. It's ideal to make them shareable on social media, too.

Make your page names and titles appealing and catchy. People love lists, and odd numbers seem to work better than even numbers. So, a "Top 7 Reasons For" or "Top 5 Tips" list is a great start for generating engaging content and boosting your SEO.

It's much easier to get people to "like," share, and link to great content, so put some effort into your site at the start and produce informative, valuable, and engaging content.

Create Content That Sells

Making content that reviews products or helps shoppers make buying decisions is the most valuable type of content. Think about including videos and buying tutorials that make you sound like and expert and add valuable insight.

Content Marketing
By: Oliver Roup, CEO, VigLink

Content driven commerce, as suggested here, is a growing area of business, however, it's a sector whose growth relies on good copy creation and an engaged audience. Building a sizable and loyal audience is the core challenge for content creators. So, my advice for all content makers is to one, find your niche and stick with it (this defines your brand), establish a direct relationship with your audience, and then consider monetization opportunities that enhance these.

Native advertising—the notion that monetization is integrated into your site's core experience—is generally preferred. Banner ads programs such as AdSense, while a healthy revenue stream, don't quite enhance your site and should be used judiciously. The best approaches to monetization will complement or enhance your content, not the other way around. A good question to ask of any monetization program is, "does this monetize my content or the just white space around my content?"

At VigLink, we've built an easy way to add native monetization into most types of content. We monetize on the content itself by focusing specifically on normal links within content. We can automatically affiliate links you already have or insert new affiliated links when we detect mentions of products, brands, and retailers. For those with a heavy social media presence, we can also affiliate links shared via these platforms.

Link-based native monetization is the natural method for monetizing content-driven commerce. Still, we often see content creators sending enormous amounts of traffic to merchants while receiving no compensation. Most fall into two camps—they are simply unaware of the affiliate marketing opportunity (luckily, that's not you!), or they pass up the additional revenue citing the time involved in setting up and managing affiliate relationships. The key is automation. What can take hours of ongoing maintenance every week is done in a few minutes with a program like VigLink.

In the end, this lets you focus on building better content and developing the relationship with your audience. Without these, no monetization will work as well as it could.

Public Relations Drives Traffic, Conversions, Sales & Data Acquisition

By: Parker Powers, Co-Founder & CEO, Millionaire Network

Public relations is perhaps one of the most under utilized, low-cost and high ROI forms of marketing there is and it's amazing what a good ole' fashioned press release can do when strategically inserted into the public conversation.

For example, in 2006, two days before Valentine's Day, I built a dating entertainment site in only 48 hours called iBreakUp.net. The idea was that, Internet dating was now a $1+ Billion dollar a year business, so I wanted to offer the public the first online service to dump those online relationships with ease—that was the controversy. I ponied up a few bucks for a press release and distributed it across the wire on Valentine's morning, and the $299 ended up landing my idea on the homepage of Yahoo, which ended up equaling a massive amount of earned media.

30,000 people ended up using the service in the first seven days, and it garnered major radio play from Howard Stern to the Bob & Tom show. Can you buy that kind of advertising? Not for that amount of money. The dating data alone generated an astronomical ROI and converted like crazy in response to offers in that vertical.

Making a Press Release That Works

Anyone who works in the PR world knows that there are right and wrong ways to go about press releases if you want this type of strategy to work. Picking your angle is one of the most important things you can do—does the product work with a human-interest angle? Does it help make lives easier? Is it controversial? What aspects help make it unique? It's important to not base the article on the product you are promoting otherwise you could be directed to the sales team. And, just as importantly, never write anything you can't back up.

Press Release 101

If you're not familiar with writing an actual press release and you'd like to give it a go, rather than hiring a firm, there are basic PR 101 rules.

1. **Length**—A typical press release is between 300-500 words.
2. **Quality**—An intriguing headline, proper paragraphs, and grammar can all be lumped into quality. Be sure that your writing is top notch and there are no grammatical errors.
3. **Add Quotes**—Use quotes in your press release without over selling the product. Again, there's a fine line between promoting a product/service and telling a story that includes the product/service, etc. Shoot for the latter.
4. **Send Your Press Release to Specific Sources**—Know your audience and where it should go.

If you're in affiliate looking to get a product out there, drive traffic and conversions; creating a strong press release is a powerful and unique way to do so.

Link Development

People will link to great content simply because it's great content. People will also link to content that is fun or funny. Why should people link to your content? Search engines like websites that people link to from quality sites. What search engines don't like are sites that have lots of poor quality links and/or buy links.

Getting Links From Bloggers

When thinking about getting links from bloggers, remember that the more relevant the blog, the better the traffic is that's clicking on the links, and the more relevant the information, the more like that search engines will find it. Think about the mindset of the blogger you're approaching—bloggers want great content that their readers will find interesting and end up sharing. The best way to approach bloggers is at an event in person. Try linking up and sharing their content on social media, as well as making comments on it—quite simply, present yourself as a real person. Write to bloggers and ask if you can do a guest post for them, this is one easy to accomplish that. If you do a guest post for someone, they will normally include a link back to you in the post. Put this in the post you send them, but don't ask for links—if you do, they might think that you are just after links and end up ignoring you.

Getting Links From Advertisers

Yes—if you make great content, advertisers may well link to you! Links from advertisers can do wonders for your search engine optimization. Links from, and reviews by advertisers can also be reposted on your site and improve the visitors to your site.

Social Signals and Social Proof

Consumers and search engines are not stupid. If websites are getting lots of links on Facebook and mentions on Twitter, it's probably because lots of people like the content and trust it. Having a strong social media presence and following will help your search engine visibility and encourage people to visit your site and act on your reviews to make purchases.

Affiliate Links In Text

If you are generating a lot of text content and want to include affiliate links within the text, but don't want to have to research and keep them up with them all, you can use a service called VIGLINK. This service automatically ads affiliate links to your text.

Note: I am an advisor for this company.

Call To Action

Don't forget to enable your visitors to make a purchase. If you are going to review a product, make sure to offer your perspective at the bottom of the review, along with a clear link to the product.

Disclosure

If you are a US-based affiliate and are publishing reviews and recommendations and making money from them, you must have to disclosure statement on your site that clarifies that you are making money. If you are an affiliate outside of this US, this is still a highly recommended business practice.

Conclusion

Think about what makes your site interesting, compelling, and fun. Why should people come to your site and trust it? Why should people link to and share your content?

Chapter 8:

Landing Pages

Landing Page Optimization

Make sure the landing page is a landing page. Many people send customers to a home page that is not optimized for what they're looking for. Send people to pages that are dedicated to what they are specifically looking for.

Follow The Promotion

Make sure the landing page keeps the promise of the advertisement in the promotion. If your ad is one color and promises something like a 20% off voucher, make sure that the landing page is the same color, has that offer on it, and is easy to find.

Keep It Short and Simple

We're all strapped for time, and with social media allowing us to have more and more messaging thrown at us all the time, it's important to keep your message simple and to the point. Make sure there is no unnecessary content.

Remove Clutter and Navigation

If you're trying to get people to buy things, then they probably don't need to read the about page or navigate around your website too much. Remove the navigation and keep customers focused on the purchase. If you want to sell on Facebook, then keep the Facebook share button on the landing page. If not, move it to the thank you page and let them go to Facebook after they have made the purchase.

CTA Above The Fold

Keep the call to action above the fold, meaning that when the user opens the website, they don't have to scroll down to find the way make a purchase. If you have more information that goes below the fold, put a second call to action at the bottom of the page.

Phone Numbers

Most affiliate programs now include phone tracking and many people prefer to call rather than using other means of communication. With the rapidly growing use of mobile phones, it's become increasingly more important to include a phone number, so if that option is there, make sure to do it.

Testimonial

Having great testimonials can help improve conversions. People trust what other people have to say about products and services, especially if that person is a celebrity or a well-known authority on the topic. However, don't post falsified or made up testimonials, as you can get in legal trouble for doing so.

Keep Forms Short

If you ask people to register on your site, then keep the amount of information you collect short—a good rule of thumb is, the shorter the better. People are used to entering their name and Email address, but they are much less likely to add their phone number or sensitive information such as their social security number. If you need additional information, consider splitting the form into two pages. Once someone has filled in the first page, they're more likely to carry on. Get their Email address on the first page so that you can contact them if they do not complete the second page.

Privacy

When you fill in a form online, you often worry about receiving spam. Have a privacy policy and let users know in plain English and that you will not spam them. With a clear-cut privacy policy on your landing page, users will be more likely to trust you and give you their information.

Terms and Conditions

Just as with the privacy policy, make the terms and conditions of the site clear and easy for people to understand. If you appear to be hiding your intentions through complicated and misleading jargon, customers will simply not trust you.

Videos

Videos can show things that are not easily explained and can add a level of consumer trust that would not be there otherwise. Videos are definitely worth testing and can dramatically improve conversions.

Thank You Page

Add value on the confirmation page. If you've had someone register, the least you could do is ask them to share it on social media. You could upsell other products or give them a bonus item for giving you more information.

Testing

Like every other part of the affiliate process, constant testing is important. Changing the color of a button can make all the difference to your campaign. Keep testing and changing things to get the maximum returns possible from your traffic. Remember, over time your traffic sources may change and you will need to change your landing page with them.

Tools

There are a variety of tools that can help you with landing page optimization, from simple A/B testing to changing out all of the elements of the page.

Professional Designs

If you're going to ask people to give you their personal information, you need them to trust you. The more professional the design looks, the more likely customers are to trust you.

Conclusion

Remain focused on why visitors are coming to your page. Figure out how you can get them to the sale or lead page as efficiently and effectively as possible, while still keeping the promise from the original advertisement.

Chapter 9:

Competitive Intelligence

Competitive intelligence is the practice of gathering and analyzing data about your competitors. The goal is to maximize your opportunity for success, reduce risks, and maximize profits. What you don't know could be hurting your profits a lot, and learning from your mistakes takes time and costs money. So, save time and money and learn from other peoples' successes with competitive intelligence tools. Although competitive intelligence also takes some time and effort to figure out, finding and utilizing the best tools you can afford will increase your chances of success.

Reasons to Use Competitive Intelligence

1. Measure your success versus the success of your competitors.

2. Avoid being caught by surprise with market shifts and stay up to date with current industry trends.

3. Prevent wasting your time and money by doing things ineffectively.

4. Spot gaps in the marketplace and targeting those potential areas for growth.

5. You only know what you know—competitive intelligence can provide information that you don't have.

Expanding Your List of Competitors

It's not always easy to know whom you're competing with and who is fighting for the same traffic. Competitive intelligence tools can help you to expand your list of competitors and rule out others.

Review Google and Bing Ads and Keywords

If you're going to setup a campaign for buying clicks, knowing how someone else is doing it can be incredibly valuable information—in the end, it will save you a lot of time and money. With something like follow.net and other similar tools, you can put in the URL of a site that you're interested in and it will show you a list of the keywords that are being bid on, as well as the ads they are running and how frequently those ads are being run. You can also see the sites that show their ads if they're using content networks to drive traffic, too. Using this information can help kick start your own campaigns, or help you improve your existing campaigns.

Landing Pages

Beyond learning what ads and keywords your competitors are using, you can also see what landing pages they're driving traffic to. This will show you what campaigns the competition is running and what offers they see as profitable.

Content Development Research

You can enter your competitor's URL and find the key phrases that are ranking well for them, what traffic those phrases are getting, and how competitive those phrases are. You can use this to create your own content strategy. Focus on valuable keywords that target users and that are easy to rank for.

Link Building Strategies

Along with learning the types of content and key phrases that your competitors are ranking, for you can also see what sites link to them from which terms. This will provide you with a list of sites that may be easy targets to get links from.

Traffic Trends

It's also possible to see how much traffic your competitors are getting over time. Look for sites that are rapidly increasing in traffic and try and find out why they are being so successful.

Referring Sites

Yes, you can see where your competitors are getting their traffic, and can be used as key potential traffic sources for your own site. Make sure to research the terms that those sites are ranking for and why those visitors are going to that site. Their referring sites could be great sites for you to do deals with and get traffic.

Competitors

If you find an advertiser that you want to promote but don't have much information on their competitors, you can use competitive intelligence tools to help you identify competitors and ultimately find more fruitful affiliate programs to promote. You may also find other traffic sources that they are not exploiting and identify an affiliate program that you want to run. If you see a site that you like and want to make something similar, you can review all the competitors and spot possible gaps in the market.

Exit Sites

You can see where the traffic from your competitors goes. This is a potential list of sites to advertise on and work with. Sometimes users don't buy instantly and if you can offer them a better alternative, you can capture the interest of someone that you know is close to purchasing.

Review Their Affiliate Programs

If you find an advertiser you like, research the networks that they are on and what the payouts are in order to make sure you are getting the best deal you can. This will also be a great place to find affiliates driving them traffic and will possibly offer some inspiration for you to make your own sites.

Demographics

Demographic information on advertisers will tell you if the traffic you have is likely to convert for their specific offer. Reviewing the demographic information of sites that you want to buy traffic on compares to the demographics of affiliate programs that you want to run and will help you decide whether or not the traffic will convert. It will also give you guidance for making content for your affiliate sites. You can get a variety of details on visitors, including age, sex, income, family, etc.

Social Media

Even if you're not planning on using social media to promote your site or offer, it's worth reviewing the social media conversation. Activity on social media may inspire new content creation or terms to bid for, or at the very least, give you insights into what types of offers are working well at the moment. If you notice that bloggers or other publishers are talking about an advertiser, then you might be able to find an untapped audience or an upcoming market trend.

Alerts

Research should not be a one-time thing. Setting up alerts to see when someone changes their PPC campaign will tell you what they think is working and what is not. Setup alerts to make sure this information is sent to you.

Conclusion

The most important aspect of competitive intelligence is knowing how to use the information to make money. Start out with some key questions about your offers or advertisers, find the right tools for you, and learn as much as you can about your competitors and your specific offer. The more knowledge you have about industry trends and the specifics of your campaign, the easier it will be to hone in on practices that will make your program successful.

Chapter 10:

PPC With Google and Bing

PPC with Google

PPC, in general, has a lot of similarities, however, each different platform has its own little nuances. So before you get too in-depth, it will be helpful for you to understand the basics.

- Landing pages
- Keyword research
- Creating ad copy

1. Landing Pages

In Google, you will be issued a quality score on your ad. There are three components that determine quality score—the ad, keywords, and landing pages. The key here is relevance. This score is a numerical value between 1 and 10—one being the lowest and ten being the highest.

To offer an example, let's say that you're looking to buy a red tie. You're going to enter the search term "red tie" in the search engines. You'll click on an ad that contains "red tie" in it somewhere (Google bolds search terms wherever they appear on the page, including the ads). You will want to land on a page (hence, the term "landing page") that sells red ties. Google would look at this ad experience as relevant and will issue a quality score accordingly.

You need to be writing ads that have a high click-through rate (CTR). This has been one of the biggest indicators of quality score for my ads. Google is looking at the interaction that is occurring after the click, so if you're writing ads that have a high CTR, but those visitors bounce back to Google 2 seconds later, then your Quality Score may suffer.

You'll want to make sure that those who click on your ads are staying on your landing page and moving to other pages. If you have Google analytics set up, then you can see what your landing page's bounce rate is.

There are some benefits to achieving high quality scores. Those with high quality scores tend to be more successful, experience a lower cost per click, more clicks overall, and higher ad positions.

If the ultimate goal is to increase and maximize conversions, concentrating on how the buyers will respond right after clicking on a paid advertisement is crucial. As for those who manage websites, having enough targeted traffic is significant, however, for business longevity, trades, and sales, conversions are a must and any possibility to improve should be regarded as such.

Hence, if the ad assured a wonderful offer to save income and soon after clicking the advert, visitors are taken to a homepage that needs time to locate the offer, i.e. locating the right page, this will considerably minimize any possibility of generating new sales and also leave a bad impression about your company in the buyer's mind

That's why the consumer's experience needs to match what was presented in the actual advertisement and care should be taken when managing your Pay Per Click marketing campaigns.

A squeeze page will have several uses, but employing a few main strategies will make it easy to create landing pages that will bring sales. To get started, make sure that each squeeze page includes a distinctive selling point. Ask yourself what's unique about your product; what makes it different from the other products in the same niche? Provide strong reasons to your buyers so that they will be willing to buy your product. Provide all necessary details about your product/products.

So, the very first thing that needs to stand out is your title and header, as these two things grabs the attention of any potential buyer. The title is something that explains to the customer what the page is all about. So, it's highly recommended that your landing page title should match your PPC ads.

The important factors that clients and consumers look for is confidence and a user friendly experience. Thus, including customer feedback and testimonials inside the landing page can help develop confidence with future prospects by means of previous testimonials that prove that you offer top quality services and products. To further improve your chances of sales, use third party certificates to assure customers that your website is safe and secure.

Don't forget to test your different strategies. By doing different kinds of experiments, such as using different ad copies, using different titles, different layouts for your landing page, you can find the best working strategy for you that will help your business in long run.

If you're participating in an online marketing campaign, one part of that campaign is probably a pay-per-click campaign utilizing something like Google AdWords. You should remember that just because you are using the Internet as part of your marketing, the same rules, tips, and tricks apply as in the old days of sales and marketing.

One of the basic tenets of marketing and good copy writing is a "call to action." You want to tell the customer what you expect of them, not leave it up to them to wonder about your product. On the internet, one way to have a great "call to action" is to direct an online marketing campaign to a specific landing page on your website. This makes sense because you are able to direct the clients and shape how they view your product.

If you have a very specific marketing campaign lined up using specific keywords or a pay-per-click marketing campaign, then having customers land on a short-term microsite may be what works best for that campaign. The place where a pay-per-click advertising campaign has a customer directed to on your site is referred to as the landing page. There are several different types of landing pages. Think of the landing page as a one page informational piece, similar to a flyer in a newspaper, or a single sheet magazine ad. If you are running a sale for a specific product, or want to promote an event, or enter someone in a drawing or contest, a microsite might be the best option for you.

For example, for the month of March you run a full-on campaign focusing on St. Patrick's Day and how it can be your customer's "Lucky Day." Through an Internet search about your product in general, they find out about your contest. This draws them straight to your microsite pay-per-click landing page, where they find out more information about your contest before going on to the main site. On the microsite, you give them the opportunity to enter in their Email address to enter the contest. Make it easy for them to close out the window and enter your main website if the contest truly doesn't interest them—you don't want to have the microsite frustrate your customer; instead, make it seem like it really is their "Lucky Day" that they found out about your special promotional offer.

Now, because of this landing page, you were able to tell that your specific marketing campaign worked to bring in a client, and it interested them enough that they gave you their personal information in the form of their Email address. The landing page can tell them all the information they need to know about a new product or special, without the distractions that often turn off customers as a part of a larger web site. But at the same time, you aren't overwhelming them with too many graphics that keep them from getting to your web site if they still would like to experience more.

2. Keyword Research

Keyword research can be the most important piece in the online marketing puzzle. There are a number of places you can conduct keyword research. Some of these include:

- Google Keyword Tool
- Market Samurai
- WordTracker

The Google Keyword Tool is free and allows you to enter a term and see up to 800 keyword variants. It also shows you how much the CPC is for that keyword and the amount of times it's being searched for on both a Global and Local basis.

What keywords do you select for your campaigns?

The answer lies in understanding that there are all sorts of different kinds of keywords. Some are broad and others are more specific. Some are called "long-tail keywords." Here's an example to illustrate this point.

Say you're selling carrots—that term itself is broad and would be very difficult to compete against the other big companies that are targeting that term. You'd be wise to add in descriptive words like:

- Organic
- Heirloom
- Southern California-grown

As you start to develop keywords that get more and more specific according to your customers desires, it is likely that your targeted keywords become longer and longer (this is where the "long-tail" comes from). Don't be overly concerned about this, because this probably means that your keywords are getting better and better at reaching the types of customers that are most likely to buy your products in the end. You will also have less competition as you get more and more focused.

Picking the right keywords is crucial. The goal is not to drive lots of traffic to your website, but rather to drive "targeted" traffic.

Generally speaking, the higher the CPC, the better the keywords. These keywords are often referred to as buyer keywords. Competition is stiff on these keywords. You want to make sure that you pick keywords that are relevant to what you have to offer.

3. Creating Ad Copy

This is where you'll need to combine technique and creativity. A little ingenuity and you're on your way! Let's first discuss some technique for ad copy. First, the keyword should be present in the ad, whether that's in the headline or the body— copy is entirely up to you. Remember that the keyword will be bolded by Google wherever it appears on the page.

We've found it extremely beneficial to put the keyword in the headline, as that's what people typically see first. Always keep in mind the goal of the ad—to get someone to click on the ad and move forward in the sales process or sales funnel. The body copy of the ad should contain a promise. Many successful advertisers will take advantage of discounts and free giveaways; those things help their ads stand out more than the other ads on the page.

Here are some examples of such:

- Free shipping
- 70% off
- Order 12 pairs, get the 13th free
- Free flashlight included

This article will explain how PPC can take your business to the next level and beyond by harnessing the marketing power of the Internet. Most savvy businesses use or have used PPC advertising to turbo charge their businesses.

In order to take your business to the next level, you should know how PPC works. PPC is a paid form of advertising and as the name suggests, you pay every time someone clicks on your ad. On the surface this sounds like it could be an expensive exercise but there are several things to <u>keep in mind</u> when considering PPC:

1. When a person types their keywords into the search bar, search engines like Google will give them results of what they are looking for. In addition to this, there are also PPC ads on those search pages that are relevant to the keywords that the user has typed in. For example, they may have typed in "how PPC can take your business to the next level" and the information on this topic, plus ads offering services around this topic will pop up. The upshot of this is that the ads will be targeted to what the user is looking, for so there is more of a chance of getting willing buyers to click on your PPC ad.

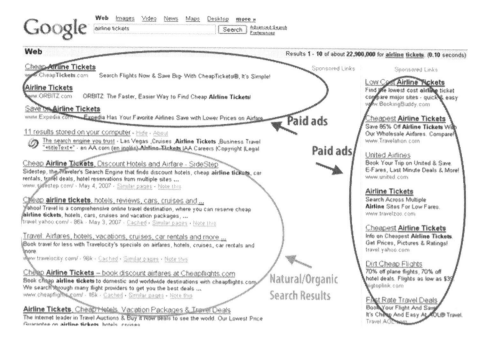

2. You nominate how much you are willing to pay every time that someone clicks on your ad. You could nominate as little as 0.01c or as much as $50 or more. Usually the price is influenced by two things—how much demand there is from advertisers for certain terms, and how important it is to be in the first three or four ads of the first page of search results. Put simply, with competitive ads you will have to be prepared to pay a lot more per click to get on the first page or your ad may never be seen. The more you are willing to pay the more chance you have of getting on the first page.

3. You can set a daily budget so that you don't blow your budget! So depending on much it costs for you to get your ad appearing high up on the search results you could have a daily budget from $5 to $1000+. This is an important area to monitor, as any successful businessperson will tell you, because if you don't control your budget then instead of learning how PPC can take your business to the next level, it could send you broke!

4. Googles AdWords program is the most popular form of PPC advertising. They allow 25 characters for the headline and two lines of 35 characters each, therefore your message has to be short and to the point, meaning that your ad has to be laser-focused. Make sure to <u>enable Google remarketing,</u> as it will help you to stalk people online. This will help your business grow by leaps and bounds.

5. You can run more than one ad so that you can experiment with different types of wording and headlines. This will help you identify what is most effective in terms of people clicking on your ads and subsequently purchasing your product or service. If you want to know how PPC can take your business to the next level, then you must remember that people clicking on your ad isn't the real measure. The real measure is how many of those people actually become buyers. You may find that an ad gets fewer clicks but it results in more buyers because the ad appeals to people ready to buy rather than appealing to people who are just browsing.

So one of the keys to how PPC can take your business to the next level is the wording of your ads. It is very important that you choose your keywords carefully. These are the words that searchers are most likely to type into the search engine. If you are in a specific market, it might be a good idea to include a location in your keywords, that way you are able to target by geography, rather than a generic, overarching product. For example, if you're a sporting goods store in San Francisco, include "San Francisco sporting goods" so that relevant, local buyers in San Francisco are able to find your business, rather than customers from other parts of the world who happen to be searching for a sporting goods store. If your product or service is not location specific then this obviously does not apply to you.

Another beneficial practice when using PPC is to include negative keywords—this means that if searchers type in certain words then your ad will not show. For example "free," "discount," "cheap" or "bargain" may be keywords that you want to avoid. If searches are after cheap or free stuff and you charge a premium, then these users will waste your PPC budget so make sure that you use negative keywords.

Furthermore, another aspect of keywords to keep in mind is the length. Generally, the shorter the keyword phrase, the more searches it will have. For example the term "men's shoes" gets 1.22 million searchers a month. If we extend the phrase to "men's shoe shops" there are 5400 searches per month and "large men's shoes" returns 8100 searches. The term "buy men's shoes online" has 1900 searches.

Of these three keyword phrases, the one most likely to result in a buyer is the third one because it is specific and it has the word "buy" in the phrase. This leads us to another important point—make sure to include the word "buy" in your ad heading if possible. This will help to filter the type of searchers that will click on your ad. Again, using our example above you could have "Buy Large Men's Shoes" as your heading. You have the search phrase in the title and you also have "buy" in there to help further filter the searchers so that it is more likely that only buyers will click on your ad. Remember that you want people clicking on your ad who are ready to buy your service or product, not just after some information.

Another trick for converting clicks into buyers is to make sure that when a searcher is taken to your website they arrive at a landing page that matches their keyword search. So if we use the men's shoes example above, if your ad says "Large Men's Shoes" then make sure your landing page says "Large Men's Shoes" and not something like "Men's Sports Shoes." The more targeted your AdWords and landing pages are, the more likely you are to get a sale.

A simple way for you to be successful in learning how PPC can take your business to the next level is to <u>look at what other companies in your industry are doing with their PPC campaigns</u>. Start by finding out what companies are the most successful because these are the ones who have learned how to optimize PPC campaigns. Once you've identified companies that are running successful PPC campaigns, study their ads, click on them, and carefully look at their landing pages. When you're viewing their ads and landing pages, look at them as a potential buyer. Ask yourself questions like what caught your eye, what words or phrases encourage you to buy, are the ads and landing pages attractive to the eye and do they draw your attention to the product or service that you're looking for? By studying what your competitors are doing you can gain some valuable knowledge on how PPC can take your business to the next level.

To conclude this section on PPC campaigns, we recommend
that you first start with Google's AdWords program. Google is
the most used search engine in the world so your ads will be
seen by more eyes than any other search engine. Google
AdWords is easy to use, they provide easy to follow training
modules, you only pay for what you ask for, they provide
tracking tools so that you can see which ads are working and
which are not, in fact the Google AdWords program makes the
whole process of learning how PPC can take your business to
the next level a very simple process. You do have to do a <u>bit of
work to begin</u> with but it will not take you long to get up to
speed, so we would encourage you to give Google AdWords a
shot so that you can quickly and successfully learn how to run
PPC campaigns.

If you would like to master keyword research and learn more
about its importance to your online business, then continue
reading. Later on will be talking about the significance of low
competition and long tail keywords, and the best way to easily

discover them. After reading this, you should be capable of doing keywords research like a professional.

Long Tail Keywords

Long tail keywords are important to your online success. Long tail key terms are keywords having three or more words. Based on research, 80% of all <u>queries are long tail</u>. These search phrases are extremely simple to rank for, meaning that you can safeguard a top place with minimum effort. These long tail search phrases result in a greater conversion when compared with common keywords. These key terms are extremely advantageous in the long term for the reason that they are targeting individuals who are looking for particular information, and thus more eager to take action such as clicking on advertisements or following you by Email. Long tail search phrases are excellent for any site simply because of its low level of competition, greater conversion rate, and ability to attract more potential site visitors.

Low Competition Keywords

Unless you have an authority site with <u>1000s of back-links,</u> it is vital to target keywords that have low level of competition. If you are aiming for "weight loss", you will have to do a lot of effort, since there are thousands and thousands of other pages fighting and competing for the top spot. As a result, it's far better to target less competitive keywords such as "Green Tea Weight Loss." Keywords with low competition are suitable for fairly new sites, since it's easier to get ranked more quickly. These search phrases normally tend not to go up and down, which means your site will continue to be on top. If you are simply beginning, then I suggest searching for some of these long tail keywords with low level of competition.

How To Find Low Competition Keywords?

One more place to search can be Google's suggestion. Hopefully you have experienced this before when typing something into Google's search bar, Google will instantly try to recommend some searches that people normally do. These search phrases are categorized by popularity, which may give you an understanding of how common certain phrases are. Lastly, the most well known keyword research application is Google Keyword Tool. It may appear a little bit confusing in the beginning, however it is extremely beneficial. It shows all the search volume about those particular keyword/keywords. All you have to do is select the best one with low competition and enough search volume.

The majority of people in the world are familiar with bulk Emails and pesky pop-up ad, which interrupt our lives and Internet experiences on a daily basis, however, a new type of online-based Internet advertising strategy has recently been developed by a number of software providers. This new technique is known as pay per click advertising or PPC. There are several different providers that offer this type of software; chief among them is Google, who enters the market for pay-per-click advertising with their contribution, Google AdWords.

While this program is excellent, and easy to use and understand, Google has provided the program's users with a wide variety of tutorials, training programs, and other helpful materials, that can teach anyone vital PPC tips and PPC tricks. At the same time, private websites such as www.PPC.org are also in operation. These types of websites offer users articles, discussion boards, or contact information for professional pay per click advertising firms, which employ trained specialists, who can help small business owners create, monitor, and manage their own unique pay per click advertisement campaign. However, people who own their own small businesses cannot afford the services of professionals, and that is perfectly understandable and acceptable.

Pay per click advertising is still well within your reach. As has been previously mentioned, Google AdWords provides a great deal of helpful features that can help you create an advertising campaign that successfully utilizes nearly every aspect of Internet-based advertising. First of all, pay-per-click advertising software includes features that allow users to specifically target their desired demographic groups based on ethnicity, age, gender, and personal interests. At the same time, pay per click advertising software also utilizes standard search engine optimization techniques based on keywords set by the user, which can not only make it quite easy for prospective customers to find information on your products and services, but can also help increase your company's rank within search engines such as Google and Bing.

Furthermore, these programs allow users to track the number of visitors to their websites, and also the amount of visitors who eventually become clients. Based on this information, pay per click advertising has rewritten the rules of the game. Years ago, business owners had to use separate programs in business arrangements to achieve such a multifaceted Internet-based advertising campaign. Now, all of these features are available through a single set of software programs.

When considering the matter of website advertising, you need to understand that you have plenty of strategies at your disposal. You will need to decide what tools to use and understand that those tools must suit your business' demands and specifications. If you are an individual who is interested in an excellent paid marketing option, then you cannot make a mistake with employing PPC advertising for your marketing campaign. Ask yourself what you anticipate to gain from PPC advertising? What are the downsides of using this marketing channel? Continue reading for answers to all your questions.

Advantages

There are several benefits of using PPC advertising for your e-commerce business—for one, it is undoubtedly among the quickest methods to get your advertising message to thousands of individuals. You will only need to create your account and within few minutes, your PPC ads will start showing and potentials users will be able to discover them immediately—with PPC advertising, you can get instant results. PPC advertising is also extremely targeted which implies that it can bring highly potential site visitors that have a high intent to buy your product or service.

Disadvantages

Now that we've examined the positives, let's consider the shortcomings of PPC advertising. Probably one of the most prominent disadvantages of using PPC is the amount of competition. Because of its usefulness, this advertising model has become extremely popular, and because PPC's base relies on its bidding process, it becomes considerably challenging to compete for competitive keywords or phrases. Along with that, if a PPC advertising campaign becomes too large, handling it becomes significantly more complicated, despite the fact that it's relatively easy to set up. Moreover, this PPC costs much more in comparison to other advertising channels.

Final Words

Similar to other marketing techniques, PPC has its pros and cons. Given that you're aware of advantages and disadvantages of PPC, you should know at this point if this specific method will go well with your business or not. PPC is a remarkably flexible approach that could produce outcomes swiftly and is extremely recommended for online business owners.

PPC with Bing

Google AdWords is the "big boy" in the PPC advertising space, capturing the majority of the search-marketing ad spends. However, Bing search accounts for 30% of the search market share in the US search landscape, and in the past year alone they have taken an additional 5% of the search market. If you're wanting 100% of all the available searches, Bing Ads is a must and smart addition to your marketing mix.

Having said that, let's talk about some things that will help you. Here are the areas that will be covered:

- Budget
- Analytics
- Mobile vs. Desktop
- Negative Keywords
- Quality Scores
- Local Extensions

1. Budget

When you're starting Bing Ads, don't go and blow your budget in the first month. Take it slow and easy. Start with a three-month budget for online paid search ads and spend evenly. If you have a $3,000 budget, plan on spending $1000 per month for each of the three months—don't spend it all in the first month.

2. Analytics

You've got to be tracking everything. You can do this through Google Analytics, which is a free program that's easy to install. What do you want to track? Make sure you tag the destination URL's of your ads to segment the Bing Ads traffic into the paid search reporting within your analytics program. Failing to do this will group the Bing Ads traffic in with the organic traffic and give you an inaccurate picture of your paid advertising program.

To learn how to tag your destination URL, visit this page: https://support.google.com/analytics/answer/1033867?hl=en &rd=1

3. Mobile vs. Desktop

You need to be able to separate the two to see what's working. Some business concepts don't convert very well on mobile. As a result, they shouldn't be advertising on mobile devices. On the other hand, some businesses convert exponentially better on mobile than on desktop.

How will you know if you aren't separating them?

Create different campaigns for mobile and desktop—it's pretty easy if you just copy the whole campaign and target it only to mobile. Make sure that when you copy over the campaign, you take off mobile ads on the desktop version.

You don't want to be bidding on the same keywords with different campaigns. When doing this I like to personally put (d) and (m) at the end of a campaign to keep track of them— (d) is for desktop and (m) is for mobile). Once you know which one is converting you won't need to worry about the other.

4. Negative Keywords

Negative keywords help you reduce your costs, increase your ROI, and reach the most interested customers. By using negative keywords, you're ensuring that your ad won't appear when specific terms are entered into the search engines.

When selecting these keywords, make sure you choose search terms that are similar to your keywords, but indicate that searchers are actually looking for a different product.

For example, if you're selling glasses, then you wouldn't want your ad to show up when people enter terms like "champagne glasses" or "drinking glasses." Those search terms are irrelevant to what you're selling.

5. Quality Scores & Quality Impact

Bing and Google do their quality scores different. The range is still between 1 and 10, where 10 is the highest. The difference is that Google penalizes your ad by giving it a lower ad position when there's a low quality score.

Bing excels in this department, as they actually teach you how to improve your quality score. They will categorize your quality score issues in one of three ways:

- Keyword Relevance
- Landing Page Relevance
- Landing Page User Experience

Quality Impact is a relatively new feature of Bing Ads that will tell advertisers how many new impressions they stand to gain by improving their quality scores. There are three rewards:

- Gain less than 100 additional impressions a day.
- Gain between 100 and 500 additional impressions a day.
- Gain more than 500 additional impressions a day.

On many occasions, this has helped me prove to clients that we need to work on putting keywords on landing pages and improve site speed.

To learn more about quality impact, visit this link:

http://community.bingads.microsoft.com/ads/en/bingads /b/blog/archive/2012/10/31/introducing-quality- impact-a-new-way-to-measure-the-impact-of-quality- score-2.aspx

6. Local Extensions

Everything is turning local—start using location extensions to leverage and drive all the local traffic to your business. In April 2011, Forrester Research report found that 70% of consumers research products online and then purchase offline—you want to be there when this happens. It's pretty simple to setup, just enter your business address, campaign information and you're ready to go.

You can read a full post on how to set this up, by visiting the following:

http://community.bingads.microsoft.com/ads/en/bingads/b/ blog/archive/2012/03/01/drive-local-leads-with-location- extensions-in-microsoft-advertising-adcenter.aspx

Using location extensions helps ads attain click-through rates between 8% and 16% higher than campaigns without location extensions—don't miss out on this.

How does it work? Ads with local extensions will show your business address, city, and phone number underneath the ad copy.

I've been doing a bit more with Bing Ads over the past couple months and I really like their service. I've even received phone calls from them asking if I need anything. I highly recommend them with all their recent improvements and impression share metrics. I get asked all the time about Bing Ads and how to get started—it's pretty simple. In this post I will teach you how to sign up for Bing Ads in about 30 seconds!

1. Go to <u>Bingads.com</u> and click Sign Up:

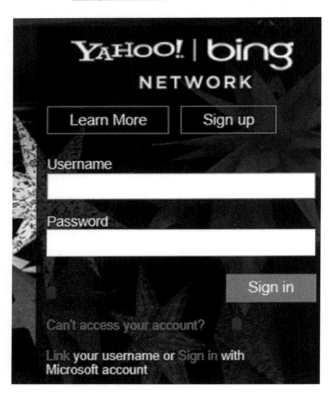

2. Next fill out the setup form. (Note: username = yourpersonalusername) (Note 2: Make sure to select 'Agency or Sales House' under the 'Industry' drop down)

3. Once that is complete, under "Accounts & Billing," click "payment methods" and add your credit card.

These steps are pretty easy and should only take about 30 seconds to do.

Chapter 11:

Facebook Ad Buying

There are two different kinds of Facebook ads available to you—303x308 pixel ads and Sponsored Stories. The 308x308 pixel ads are the ones most commonly used. They show up on your Facebook newsfeed on the right sidebar.

The key elements of this ad are the headline, the image, and the body copy. Interestingly enough, people look at the image first, the headline second, and the body copy last.

How do you create a Facebook ad?

In the Google Chrome Webstore, you can download Facebook's Power Editor. This allows you to edit and create advertisements from your browser. The other way you can create an ad is from your Facebook page.

Let's talk about Sponsored Stories now—these are a bit different than the ads we just talked about.

There are several interesting things about these types of advertisements. One, they show up in the Facebook newsfeed, and two, they display "Likes," comments, and shares.

How do you write a Facebook ad that converts well?

Images need to stand out—you can do this by adding a colored border to your picture, adding text to the picture, and using arrows that point to the body copy.

Headlines need to speak to your ideal customer. If say you're promoting an offer that's for dog owners, for example, address the dog owner by saying something like, "Attention Dog Owners!" Another popular headline technique is asking your customers a question. In the above picture, you'll notice that the ad is speaking to someone that would need leads and asking a question at the same time.

In the body copy portion of the ad, your goal is to sell the customer on why they should click your ad. It's effective to contain a call to action. In the girlfriend ad above, the advertiser used the "Click here to find out more now!" call to action. In the Biz Books ad example, the advertiser used the "Read four chapters here!" call to action.

Use the following exercise to come up with a promise for your ad:

"If you click, I promise to give you ___".

Maybe this change happened a while back and I never noticed, but it appears that Facebook Ads change to a 1-minute refresh rate. What does this mean for advertisers? Well, it means that you're paying for a 1-minute impression, and then it's gone. Is this setting advertisers up for failure?

Previously, Facebook advertising had allowed an impression where as long as you didn't refresh the page the ads would show. The average person spends 11 minutes on Facebook each day. That means that if they aren't doing anything but watching their Facebook news feed that they are seeing over 88 different ads during that 11-minute period.

Another change that Facebook has made is its ads have gone from 5 to 8 advertisements on the news feed. What this means for advertisers is that your ads need to stick out. If your ads aren't showing and standing out above all other ads then you're probably not going to get the results you're looking for.

Test, Test, Test

If you take a look at the ads to the side of this post, you will notice that they stand out much more than most other ads. It's the ones with a red box around the outside. I've done many tests on colors outside the picture and have have found that people are 20% more likely to click on the ads if it has a red box on the outside. I've also found that yellow gets an 11% increase in CTR. This can mean the difference between profitability and failure. The point here—you should always be testing to find ways to increase your clicks and conversions.

Red vs. Yellow Box

Yes, I've tested this and these were the two box colors that tested the best. The CTR of red was 20% better than the average ad. The CTR of the yellow was 11% more. Something interesting to note is the red also had a 5% conversion on the back end to a completed sale.

In my opinion, the top ads have a red box around them, although that could be different for each product—either way, it's something you should be testing. You should be testing everything that you do. Make sure that you're ads are being clicked on, find the right picture that converts better than the rest, then choose a box color around the picture and it will help your CTR and most likely your conversions on the back end!

Best of luck getting the most out of your Facebook Ads!

We learn by example rather than just listening to someone talk, so this section is going to focus on Facebook ads that have recently caught my attention. Some of these even caused me to purchase products that advertisers were selling. It's important, as an advertiser, to always be on the look for great ads. As we examine these ads, I will teach you how to create winning Facebook ads. When you apply the following concepts, you'll dramatically improve your CTR (click-through-rate):

- Flagging your prospect
- Applying the 'curiosity' hook
- Relevant picture to the ad
- Free download, white paper, eBook, etc.

1. Example of Flagging Your Prospect

I took this screenshot a while back, as it is a great example of flagging your prospect. In this particular ad, Fiverr is targeting people interested in purchasing cheap and easy SEO gigs. When you flag a particular customer, you should be designing a message that is narrowly targeted to them.

Here are some words that you can use when attempting to flag:

- Attention
- Struggling
- Mentioning the specific product, interest, service, need or desire

2. Example #2 The 'Curiosity' Hook

Nobody "Likes" Your Page?

We couldn't get 'Likes' either... until we made this one small "tweak" to our page.

I love this Facebook ad and I call it the "curiosity" ad. These ads are proven to get clicks. A person seeing this ad is curious and wants to know this "tweak," because they believe it will get them more Facebook likes. I believed it and it led me to click the ad to learn the tweak.

Words you can use to get people curious:

- Formula
- Secret
- Blueprint

3. Relevant Pictures, Landing Pages & Descriptions

This is a surefire way to make sure your ads either get approved or declined. They want to know if both your ad description and landing page are relevant. I have seen several irrelevant landing pages from AppSumo. While they know how to run really interesting ads, their landing pages say nothing about the ad copy and make you opt-in. It is irritating and actions like that increase your chances of getting declined, not to mention really low conversions—if they even make it that far.

4. Free Download, White Paper, eBook, etc.

My friend Laura Roeder created this ad, and she's done a terrific job illustrating the point I'm about to make—she's offering a free report. I did, however, have to opt-in to receive it, but the landing page sold me on the benefits of this free report. Ads like this do a terrific job of building your Email list and getting a high CTR.

Recently, I was tasked with developing a Facebook marketing strategy for a video marketing consulting program, and the following steps are exactly what I followed to make it a successful Facebook campaign.

1. What Is The Message of Your Fan Page?

The goal of your Facebook fan page is to create a community around a single topic and message. This message will be present when you're doing the daily activity that you'll learn about shortly. Your fans will respect you when they see that you're only talking about one topic.

2. Daily Marketing Activity.

It's a sad truth that Facebook doesn't show your updates to every single one of your fans. This change occurred after they created their "Edge Rank" algorithm. To combat this problem, you want to make sure that you're keeping your reach up and getting activity on your updates.

Activity is defined as likes, shares, and comments. To keep your reach up, you want to make sure that you're updating your page with content at least 3 to 5 times a day.

What kinds of content do you want to share?

You have a choice between textual statuses, pictures, videos, and blog posts. Facebook values pictures and uploaded videos more than any of the other options. Did you know that videos uploaded to Facebook stay in the newsfeed 10 times longer than a YouTube link? That buys you more time to get additional likes, comments, and shares on the video.

3. Getting More "Likes."

There are essentially <u>three ways to go about getting more likes</u>. First, understand that if your content goes viral due to people sharing it, then you'll scoop up additional likes. Second, you want to create a valuable giveaway. Using an attractive giveaway acts as bait that will entice people to like your page in order to receive it.

Making this happen can be rather tricky, as a lot of things come into play here. You'll need an auto-responder service to deliver the giveaway, an opt-in form, and a tool to create custom fan page tabs. There are hundreds of auto-responder services out there and tools to make custom tabs. Do your due diligence and find one that works for you.

To put all this together, you'll need to create a Facebook ad that targets your ideal fan and entices them to like your page in order to receive your valuable offer. To learn more about Facebook ads, visit <u>http://ppc.org/category/facebook-ads/</u>.

The thing that makes this powerful is that you're building your Email list as well as getting likes for your fan page. Every marketer will tell you that the money is in the list. I'd like to add that it's in the targeted list. It's targeted because you're targeting specific people with specific interests when you are creating your Facebook ad.

4. Utilizing The Power of Sponsored Stories.

The ad process above is for a typical 308x308 pixel ad that you see on the right sidebar of your Facebook newsfeed. A sponsored story is different in budget, what you can promote, where they appear, and the display of activity or "social proof."

Sponsored stories show up in the news feed and show the amount of activity it's received (social proof). Sponsored stories give you two budget options—the plain option gives you a choice to promote it for any multiple of 5 in the range of $5 to $50, the second option allows you to promote up to $300 with extra targeting such as age and location.

Using sponsored stories will help you scoop additional likes as they are shown to fans and friends of fans. While running sponsored stories, I've found that it gets shown to people who don't really care about the story—you assume that risk and it does happen.

5. Be Consistent and Split Test.

You need to be consistent with daily activity, sponsored stories, and advertisements. Take the weekends off if you want, but be back at it Monday morning. Whenever I take a few days off I watch my reach plummet into low and unacceptable numbers—the more consistent you are, the more you communicate to others that you're serious about your business. Consequently, you'll have a much larger and noticeable impact.

You'll need to be split testing the aspects of your ads (pictures, ad copy, and landing pages) in order to reach the optimal and desired levels of success.

In another Facebook Ads case study, we'll show a real world example of a Facebook campaign that worked for Tareas Plus, an EDU site that's helping people to learn mathematics and physics. I recommended that clients start doing Facebook Ads in order to get their online social media profiles going, and I personally think this is going to be huge for SEO in the future (though it's showing very positive signs right now). Here is the test that we did.

- **Test**: $500 Facebook budget for 3 Days for a total budget of $1500.
- **Pushing**: Posts and site traffic.

- **Goal**: Increase interactions, gain traffic, increase brand awareness, and make money.

We started with a $500 Facebook budget and wanted to test this for 3 days. Although this may seem like a lot of money to most of you, if you're spending $20k+ in AdWords or Bing Ads, you're already spending much more than that, in fact, you're spending that daily. We promoted a few videos and posts that we wanted to promote and went all in for 3 days. Here is our site traffic during those days.

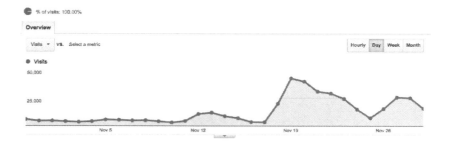

As you can see, we ended up having a spike in traffic over that day, going from 5-10K unique visits a day to almost 50K uniques in one day. The traffic did taper off the following two days, but as you can see Facebook traffic can be huge.

Another item to check out is that we had 4,849,280 impressions in one day—that's almost five million people that saw our ad and were exposed to our client's brand. If you aren't using this as another way for 5 million people to see your brand and proving that to your client, you're not thinking right. That's a ton of people that will know and/or recognize your brand, meaning that next time they see your ad they, will remember who you are.

Note: I don't recommend running $500 in sponsored posts and in Facebook ads the whole time. It will give good increases in traffic from time to time, but not every day. You also need to have 2,000+ Facebook Fans to be able to promote with Sponsored Stories.

Facebook Ads have helped Tareas Plus and several other companies that we work with to get a large increase of customers coming to their websites. Give it a try or check out all the other Facebook Ads posts that we have! Only time will tell if we can really trust all the impressions that Facebook is giving us, but for now Facebook ads are working, and working well! Not to mention people from Facebook have a 20% lower bounce rate then Google organic traffic.

After we showed these numbers to our client, they told us to keep going and gave us a $2,000 dollar budget a month for Facebook Ads. This has helped their business grow 10x over the past couple weeks.

Getting leads for your MLM business has never been easier. Maybe you don't care about MLM, but any good business appreciates a good lead. If you're not setting up your ads correctly, you can wind up spending a whole lot of money and not have much to show for it. The objective of this post is to quickly share how to get an ad up so that you can begin generating leads for your MLM or whatever business you're in.

Once you follow these four steps, you will get MLM ads using Facebook ads.

1. Create A Landing Page

Me personally, I use a system to generate capture pages quickly and easy. When you're making the capture pages, your primary goal should be to quickly get the name and Email (and possibly phone number) of a visitor. My landing pages have a title that flags my prospect and a quick sentence that gives a visitor a benefit for opting into the list.

Anything else needs to be carefully analyzed. Certain things distract a user from opting in. Examples include:

- Navigation buttons
- Excessive content
- Ads, etc.

2. Create The Ad

This step is extensive, so make sure to follow these steps:

- Choose a Facebook destination or enter a URL
- Create Headline & Text
- Insert an image

For the first step, put in the capture page that you're sending the traffic to. Next, it's time to create your headline and text.

For the headline, I flag my prospect and hit a button. In this case I'm targeting network marketers in a specific company and offering them a solution to their struggles (ending their struggle is the button).

The text contains the sentence that is actually displayed on my landing page. When you include content that is on the actual landing page, the Facebook approval rate increases dramatically. They want to see that the ad and the landing page are relevant and matched up.

3. Choose Your Audience

Again, my audience is a specific network marketing company. The targeting on Facebook is one of the reasons I prefer them to Google Ads, not to mention that the window of sending traffic to affiliate offers is still available on Facebook (subject to change).

Let's say I'm targeting the MLM company Nu Skin—this ad will be displayed to anyone who either puts Nu Skin in their statuses or they like the Nu Skin business Facebook page. This means that they are likely to be a fan of the products or they are a current distributor.

The ages I target are between 35-55. After running ads and testing them, this seems to be the audience that has money and is willing to purchase things that will help their business.

4. Budget

To see if something works, you need data—not just a day or a week, but more like 2-4 weeks of data. I run my ads continuously, analyze the data, then make necessary changes. When I select my budget, I do $10 a day and choose the CPC model. Once I find a winning ad and I'm willing to spend more, then I'll switch to a CPM model.

If you follow these 4 simple steps, <u>I guarantee</u> that you will get MLM leads using Facebook ads.

Chapter 12:

Other Media Buying

http://ppc.org/horrible-remarketing-in-expensive-ppc-niche/

It's really frustrating to see people putting up low-quality display advertising banners in an expensive niche, so this segment will delve into horrible remarketing in expensive PPC niches and how to avoid it.

I have clients in the hosting niche, so I'm always paying attention to other companies and what they're doing. This is one of the remarketing ads that I spotted last week for MyHosting website.

Can you see the wonderful photoshop job that they did to his neck? Who is the designer or company that let this slip though? This niche is a $10 to 15-per click niche. I'm sure this ad is converting wonderfully as far as CTR, but horribly on the back end. People want to see what company would let that picture get through.

Don't get me wrong; I'm not faulting the hosting company for putting up the banner—it's a small detail, but if you're spending the money to get your ads clicked on, make sure that you take the time to check over all your banners to make sure that they are perfect. In fact, they don't even have to be perfect, just decent looking

Note: MyHosting is a really good company with great customer service; they even made the list of Top 25 Hosting companies in the world voted on by 1000's of bloggers. I'm sure they'll take this experience, learn from it and become 10x better at PPC for it. It's a simple slip-up—we all do it.

Tips for Remarketing Banners

1. When you put up remarketing banners, check them out. Have three people sign off on the banners before they go live. This is a surefire way to ensure that nothing like the banner above goes up—something you will want to be sure of especially when you're spending a lot of money.

2. Always have two different ads running at the same time— you always want to be testing ads. I would recommend that you test two different banners for 2-4 weeks, or at least 20K+ impressions. This gives them enough time on the chopping block to really know what's going on.

3. Segregate your customers from potential customers with different remarketing campaigns. If you can dive down deeper than that, do it!

4. Try not to clutter your banners—you want a simple message on there. You should be able to sell your company in five words, so don't put more than five large words on there if possible. This isn't always possible, but try it—your ads will convert better.

5. Put a boarder around your ad, not much, but a couple pixels—this will improve your ad. I like to test out different colors. If you check out some of my Facebook Ads, you'll see that I love to test boarders on display ads. It's killer and will help your ads out tenfold.

Are you one of the millions of people that are using Google Adsense? How about some of the people that have been banned by Adsense? In this section we will look into why Google Adsense's new ad format is a horrible idea and will hurt your website.

The new ad is referred to as the half page unit, which Google is calling "brand friendly" ad units. This is horrible for people doing SEO on their websites. Google said in their press release that this ad size is one of the "top requests from publishers" last year.

Matt Cutts hates this, despite Google's display ad study show that this ad is one of the most requested and fastest growing ads out there, however, I'm skeptical about this. They are trying to get more money. Supposedly they will only show a "wide range of text and display ad inventory."

To give you an example of how big this is (note that all are scaled down):

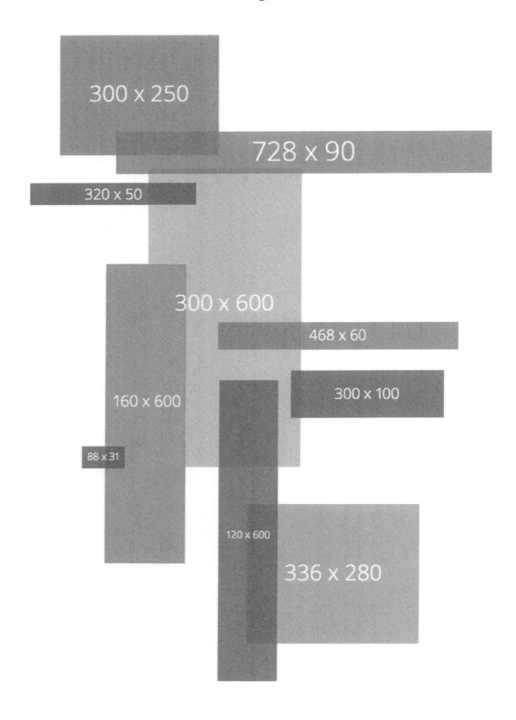

Any business that wants to get real with their online marketing needs to be remarketing itself online. You know when you go to a website then you see their ads follow you around the web, that's Google Remarketing. In this section we'll teach you why you should be remarketing your business online and how it can help you reach more customers.

Google™
Remarketing

What Remarketing Does

If you're spending money on PPC then you already know that you're spending money on your site; potentially thousands of dollars. What's the bounce rate of your site? 50-60% is typical. That means that for every 100 people you drive to your site that 60 of them will leave. Even if that number is less for PPC traffic, you're leaving tons of people on the table.

Remarketing allows Google to track everyone that comes to your site and put your ads in front of them on other sites.

If you haven't tried remarketing, you need to jump on the bandwagon—it's worth it. If you don't know how to setup a remarketing campaign, you can get a full detailed explanation on how to setup everything here.

Why Should I Be Remarketable?

After you put the snippet of code on your site you can follow anyone that came to your site to other sites that allow Google Ads and those visitors will see your ads. When they see your ads they will recognize your brand because they've been there in the past. This is a surefire way to get them to see your ads. Now you are no longer leaving people that visit your site to never return again.

People who visit your site and come back from remarketing banners are 3x more likely to purchase from you. They trust your brand; they know you. We've done tests with clients that have had up to a 5x return on spend with remarketing ads. They already know your brand so you're not pushing something new on them. The brain is much more likely to accept something it knows.

Remarketing is a way to reach out and advertise special offers to people who have already been to your site. These people can be shown different offers or promotions than people visiting your site for the first time. Not to mention that you can send them to a different page than the normal traffic.

That's not all you can do with remarketing. With remarketing you can also create lists of people who have purchased something on your site. Remarketing is a great way to send out promos and deals to those customers that purchased something on your site. You can target them individually and it's easy to setup in your AdWords account. Do this, it will help you separate everything out and get customers returning all the time.

Bottom line—you should be remarketing your business so that you're not losing out on the 50% of people that may be interested in your product but leave before they give it a fair chance.

Buying Mobile Traffic

Over the past two years the use of mobile devices to do all-things Internet has increased astronomically—evidence that our world is evolving into a mobile-dominated place. If you want some statistics to prove it, 13% of YouTube's daily views come from a mobile device. This makes up a total of up to 400 million views on mobile devices everyday.

This comes as good news for advertisers all over the world as it offers a way to expose their brands to a broader audience through new, mobile oriented ads. According to our research, customers respond better to promotions when advertisements are displayed across multiple screens.

We also found that ad recall of any product jumps up more than 74% higher for people who view the ads on TV, tablets, smartphones, and on the PC, compared to the 50% rise that is experienced by the ads if they are only viewed on TV.

We came up with a few ways that can assist you in the reach of more customers by increasing your mobile reach on YouTube.

YouTube's Promoted Video Ads on Mobile

Do you use Promoted Video ads to reach viewers searching for relevant products and potential customers browsing videos on YouTube.com? You can also use Promoted Videos to reach viewers on the go. Promoted Videos are featured at the top of the video search results on m.youtube.com, YouTube's mobile platform.

All that you have to pay is a small fee that is charged every time someone views your ad, be it on a desktop or a mobile device, all the views are put together and the counts are summarized into one complete count that will be charged on your channel. "Mobile This" are all mobile promoted ads and being that they're auction ads they are promoted by AdWords from Google+ as they are the ones in charge of promoting ads. All Google AdWords campaigns are opted into "all devices" by default, but creating separate mobile campaigns helps optimize your mobile advertising efforts and the performance of your brand channel.

YouTube Mobile Roadblocks

YouTube Mobile roadblocks give brands 100% share of voice on the YouTube home, browse, and search pages on m.youtube.com. According to recent Nielsen data, these roadblocks add 17% incremental impressions for advertisers. Adidas used mobile roadblocks to complement their homepage masthead ads. Using multiple mobile tactics in addition to roadblocks, channel views jumped 26 times over the span of their "Adidas is all in" brand campaign. This just shows the power of integrating mobile and advertising needs together.

Social Traffic

When it comes to social media, there are new ones popping up on a regular basis. The ones that garner the most traffic are (in no specific order): YouTube, Twitter, Facebook, Google +, LinkedIn, and Pinterest. One of the things that we recommend is grasping a good handle on one before moving on to another one.

Here's an SEO (search engine optimization) tip—set up your accounts with your first and last name if you can. It will rank really well if someone were to search for your name.

Example: facebook.com/johnrampton.

How do you drive traffic to your website properties using social media?

In our minds, the power of social media lies in your ability to connect with people and develop relationships. No amount of software, outsourcing, or automation can develop relationships as well as human interaction can. We recommend that you try to connect with people within your industry on a daily basis.

On Facebook, you will want to set up a page for your business. Your followers on this network are called "Likes," formerly called "Fans." To accumulate new "Likes" you'll want to follow this pattern:

- Create a valuable offer to giveaway
- Pick up an auto-responder service to both create forms and deliver the gift.
- Create Facebook ads that entice people to like your page in exchange for a like and their contact information (typically you ask for their name and Email address).

On Twitter, you can follow and be followed. You can send private messages and send @ messages, which are public for others to see. This social network is full of spammers. Relationships are king on this network, as those who don't know you will probably not click on your links. You create relationships on Twitter in a couple of ways. First, follow the person that you'd like to get to know. Second, reach out to them with a DM (direct message). Third, take the relationship to a personal level by getting on a video Skype call with that person.

On Google +, you have circles, which break down the relationship into different levels. They are:

- Family
- Friends
- Acquaintances
- Following

LinkedIn is a social network that was aimed to be a network for professionals. Build your network and share information with them. For example, share your new blog posts that you feel like your connections would benefit from. They'll visit the post if they feel like they'll stand to gain something from it.

Pinterest rose to one of the top five social media networks in the shortest period of time. As you follow people, you will see the things that they have "pinned." Those items will show up in the "home feed." As you create content on your website, you can share those articles on Pinterest. Many marketers use Pinterest to drive traffic to their websites.

A social network is only as good as the following you've built up. On the flip side, a massive following on Twitter is useless if those followers don't engage with you. The objective of this section is to teach you how to use Twitter hand in hand with your blog.

1. Customize Your Twitter.

There are a number of ways you can customize your Twitter page. They are:

- Custom background (helps people know you're the real deal).
- Describe yourself and what you're about in your Bio.
- Take advantage of the website section. You have a few different options here. You can continue the social engagement by including your Facebook URL/fan page, G+ profile, YouTube, your best converting capture page, or

your personal blog/website. You choose, but make sure to take advantage of it.

2. Engage, Engage, and Engage.

The primary way to do this is to go to Twitter.com/search. Once you've arrived at Twitter's search engine, enter a keyword that you want to see being used in the network. For example, if you enter Blogging it will return everyone that has used that search term in a tweet.

Now that you've got a list of people that are using your search term, it's time to engage with them. There are a few ways to do this:

- Ask questions
- Add to the "existing" conversation
- Follow
- RT their tweets

3. Update Frequently.

Your tweets often get buried in the millions of tweets that other users have showing up in their feed. Your Twitter "newsfeed" only shows about 15 entries until you scroll down and it shows more. Knowing that, you should be tweeting throughout the day, especially if you have a post that you want people to click and open.

4. Apply Some Copywriting to Your Tweets

When you sit down to write any post, you should be doing a little copywriting to create titles that people want to click on. Since Twitter is a micro-blog network, you only have a few characters to get your post across and get people to click any link you have in your tweets.

To get some title ideas that people want to click, I take pictures of titles that stand out to me when I'm grocery shopping, visit Cosmopolitan magazine, and read the the National Enquirer.

Those magazines know human psychology so well that they know what gets you to pick up the magazine, read it, and want to buy it.

5. Sharing Your Blog Posts

With the new Google Penguin update, Google's algorithm is placing more emphasis on social media. They value links that come from social media sites, which means that you need to be sharing your blog posts on the big social media sites. Since there are so many, I recommend you master the four largest ones: Twitter, Facebook, Pinterest, and G+.

Bored at home? Trying to find something that can be productive? Try the Tumblr blogging experience! Tumblr, founded in February of 2007, is a light blogging platform that offers a lot of multimedia sharing of items like text, photos, videos, chat, audio, quotes, and links.
Unlike the other blogging platforms, Tumblr is easy to use and user friendly. It also provides media integration with novice users and doesn't demand for extensive programming knowledge. Interaction between bloggers is simple and easy— you can just hit the follow button on the top right corner of their blog, this sends a direct message to them with the use of a built-in ask box. Tumblr also offers some features like reblog and like, wherein reblog means that a visitor can re-post any of the blog posts.

One thing that can be good with Tumblr is, it provides an easy and customizable theme design that is available in Tumblr's theme garden. Unlike the other blogging platforms, Tumblr uses a great interactive page where a user can customize a theme using the HTML language. A user just needs an ample amount of knowledge in HTML and customizing a theme will be an easy process to follow. How do you start blogging with Tumblr?

Follow These Simple Steps For a Pro Blogging Experience with Tumblr

1. Go to Tumblr.com and sign up for a new username. This username will be displayed on your Tumblr's dashboard and as an identity of your blog or url (i.e yourusername.tumblr.com or you can have your own domain). You can eventually change your username, which is available in the settings.

2. Learn how to post according to your wants. This variety of seven Tumblr blogging features will keep you right on track.

Then text. You create a post that can display images, links, and texts.

Now photos. A user can post a photo, or several photos with a variety of layouts, and descriptions. A user may upload photo/photos with the link provided.

Next quote. This consists of a box where a quote will be posted in a single-lined box for the citing of the original author.

Next link. A text linked to a website.

Next chat. Share a short or long snippet from a chat or conversation.

Next audio. A user can also post a mp3 file uploaded from the computer or a file url can be used. Only one audio is permitted a day.

Last video. Consists of an embedded video uploaded from the computer or a url from Youtube or other video sites.

3. Follow other people and get your own followers! Followers are also Tumblr blogging users. A follow can also be termed as subscribing. When a user follows you, they can see your posts on their dashboard, and if you also follow other users, their posts will show up in your dashboard. Followers can reblog, or like your posts. The more followers, the more post popularity you will get.

4. Customize your own theme. The Customize section, (yourusername.tumblr.com/customize) has everything you need to edit your theme to your liking.
Next info. Choose from the title of your blog, write your original description, and others.
Then theme. There are a lot of pre-made themes available in the theme garden. Select the html code of the one you want and paste on the HTML pane. Save and you have your theme. **Next appearance.** Change your blog's appearances. Last pages. Make a FAQ or an About Mepage using the Add page. You can also delete and edit a page.

5. Send a message. Every Tumblr's blog has an ask link, that will direct a visitor to a ask box where a message can be sent. A visitor can choose whether to publish his username or be anonymous. A new message will appear on the user's dashboard.

Follow these simple steps and you will have a great tumblr blogging experience. Explore on your own and you will definitely say, "I chose the right way to blog."

How to Make Google+ Work for You

After the initial launch of Google+, we've had the great opportunity of welcoming more than 40 million people and showing them the more than 100 features in it. This entire population of users, even after enjoying al these features, has one thing missing in their buffet, your business. Most businesses have a very good connection with their customers in the real world in real life, but have a lackluster relationship with the customers online; our objective is to let you have a good and lasting relationship with your online customers as you would in real life—this is what has led to the creation of Google+. Your business is a collection of features and products that are there to help you get closer to your customers. This will be kept at the heart of Google+ pages and will be more like an identity of your business on Google+.

On the Google+ pages you will have the ability to have real conversations with real people and not pre-arranged words by a computer. If you wish to be amazed by this phenomenon, you have to open an account on Google+ first, and after you open an account you will have the ability to post updates about your business, engage in conversations with your customers (which comes in handy for many businesses in the market satisfaction and market research area), send tailored messages to specific groups of people and see how many +1's you have across the web. Here are a few features of Google+ Pages that we think will help you build relationships:

- **Hangouts**

There are many times in which you may want to chat with your customers face to face, this comes in handy, if for instance, you are running a novel selling business or a book store—you can have an author come over for a talk on his/her book or if you are running a cosmetic shop get a beauty professional to come talk about beauty. Hangouts make this easy by letting you have high-quality video chats with up to nine customers, with a single click. You can use Hangouts to get product feedback, assist you to know how you can better your products or advertising strategies, and just simply get to know you customers. Plus, all of this is done in real time and face to face.

- **Circles**

This is a part of the new creation that allows you to organize your audience into small groups together. This makes it easy for you to share specific massages with specific groups, for instance, you could create a Circle containing people who are your most loyal customers and offer them a special discounts, or another circle of new customers and just as an incentive offer a gift for an individual who purchases the highest amount of products. This will not only increase the businesses market share, but it will also improve the relationship of the business with the consumers.

More consumers have gotten out of the TV and newspaper ages and now they are all reaching for their tablets, laptops, and smartphones for both their news and their entertainment. There has even popped up a new faction of TV watchers who are known as the light TV watchers, as they only spare two hours of their time to glance at the TV. This is true, as statistics have shown that adults between the age of 18 to 49 watch TV for less than two hours daily, which classifies them as light viewers of TV. This gap is growing day by day as new research shows that households are installing broad band Internet to their houses and up to 22% of the old TV viewers are now turning to the Internet for all their entertainment, news, and other needs.

In order to better understand how this ever-changing trend will influence advertising in 2012 and the coming years, we partnered with Nielsen to conduct over five media cross-studies to observe the patterns that people view TV and determine how effective a campaign would be. Looking at their viewing patterns on YouTube and the Google Display Network (GDN), we found that all the TV viewing has dwindled and all the light TV viewers are reached easily through cross-media campaigns such as in the case of YouTube and Google Display Network.

- **The Light TV Viewer**

The age range of these consumers tends to be between 18 to 49, most of which have high levels of education and are college-educated, high-income, social network-using, influential consumers. Our research found that light TV viewers overall averaged only 39 minutes of TV a day. Since this audience watches significantly less TV than the general population, they can be difficult to reach with TV advertising alone.

- **Additional Reach, Lower Cost**

On average, the viewing that we got on the TV campaign were added by up to 4 percent in the YouTube and Google display, and surprising enough it cost us 92% less to get this information on the Internet than the amount that it would have coasted us to get it from the TV. The research also showed that TV failed to reach 63% of light TV viewers.

- **Increased Frequency and Recall**

Finally, our research showed that online campaigns added much-needed frequency to help increase brand recall for the light TV viewer. Combining YouTube and GDN drove a 27% increase in impressions, since even light TV viewers exposed to both TV and online ads saw more online ads than TV.

Overall, the conclusive results were that it was not only cheaper to advertise in this age through the Internet, but it also showed that it's cheaper and more effective as it receives a high number of audience compared to the TV.

Creating social bookmarks is a vital tool that can assist individuals in discovering their content online without searching for it everywhere. It is also an extremely effective tool which online marketers use for creating back-links to their sites.

This section covers some of the finest websites for creation of social bookmarks, which website owners should make use of. Before talking about the social bookmarking sites, it is important to talk about social bookmark submission.

Social bookmarking websites can be used for several purposes such as:

- Creating user profiles and completing them with all necessary details along with the website URL.
- By means of social bookmarking, you can promote any excellent content material you discover online
- You may also promote your own material such as blog posts or videos.
- You can join different existing groups in your niche or you can form your own group.

There are a considerable number of social bookmark management sites out there on the Internet. The fundamental concept continues to be the same however; the themes and online communities differ from site to site.

Digg

It is the largest social bookmarking arena on the web and the communities seen on this platform are a lot more technology-driven. You can publish content material relevant to a wide range of other topics. You can however have a chance of rendering it to the home page of the website.

Delicious

Delicious is known as a labeling site more than a social bookmarking website, and is another amazing platform for creating back-links or generating targeted traffic for a website.

Reddit

Yet another social bookmarking website that has been erratic in regards to achievements despite the fact that it is among the largest and has a significant volume of website traffic.

Yahoo! Buzz

Yahoo! Buzz is presented by the Yahoo! Corporation and benefits from the massive Yahoo! community. If you are able to get to the home page of Yahoo! Buzz, you can push substantial volume of targeted traffic to your website.

Mixx

This website has not received as much consideration compared to other social bookmarking websites, however, it's still a wonderful site where you can distribute content. You may also join the communities if you would like to direct readers to your site.

Stumble Upon

This site facilitates individuals to "stumble upon" unique material that is relevant to the topic of their choice. For online marketers, this is a place to share content so that others users or webmasters can come across it.

Newsvine

Newsvine is a fantastic website for individuals who create news related stories. If you have a new website or launch a new product or service, then this is a good platform to start your marketing campaign.

Optimization

Optimization is broken down into two parts—off-page and on-page.

The goal of on-page optimization is to tell the search engines what your pages are about. Search engines are constantly evolving and looking for different things. What may have worked six months ago most likely doesn't work today. What's working today?

- **Meta Tags**—There are dozens of Meta tags. The most popular or important ones are the Title Tag and the Description Tag. Search engines display both of these tags in the search results. If you don't provide one, then they will pull data from the page and create their own.

  The Title tag should contain the keyword that the page is about. It should also be no longer than 70 characters.

  The Description tag should also contain the keyword that the page is about. You'll be safe to stay under 150 characters.

- **Image Alt Text Tag**—This tag is extremely useful, as it helps search engines know what an image is about. It also allows those with disabilities to read the image. To properly fill this out, you'll want to put the word "image" after the phrase that describes the picture.

- Another common on-page practice is putting the keyword in the first paragraph of the page. This is beneficial for visitors, as they want reassurance that they've landed on the page that will help them with the search query that they entered in.

Many marketers spam the page with their desired keyword; however, this is a mistake, as search engines want to provide the best quality experience for users. Surely you would be frustrated if a certain term kept showing up repeatedly.

Let's talk about off-page optimization now—this is where the power of search engine optimization comes in. When another website links to your website, it's known as a backlink, and sites with a lot of backlinks are typically considered to be popular websites. But, that's not always the case, as spammy marketers, known as black hat SEOs, build thousands and thousands of backlinks in hope to "game" the search engines for better rankings.

Search engines are evolving daily and are on high alert for such practices. A common and ethical way to obtain backlinks to a website or page, is through guest posting or guest blogging. This is the process whereby an author submits an article to another website in the industry. Most guest posts will contain at least one backlink to the author's website. Search engines will look at these backlinks and may possibly increase the ranking of the particular backlinked page.

Getting a website to rank in Google is not a simple task, but in this segment we will explore some things that you can do to help your site rank better.

SEO can be a rather time-consuming task, especially if you're relatively new to the process. Out of all the things that need fixing, a few stand out above the rest. Here are some of the most common issues that most business owners and entrepreneurs make when starting their site.

1. Missing Meta Description Tags

Meta information is becoming more and more useless, especially the keywords tag. Google and other search engines really like it when webmasters take the time to fill out the meta description tag. Reason being, it makes it easier for them, as they won't have to randomly pull information from the page and create a description.

Webmasters should be filling these description tags as they go along. Otherwise, you'll have hundreds, if not thousands, to fix at some point. Filling your own tags out gives you control of your content and how people view it via the SERPs. Why would you leave that up to chance by leaving it blank? Search engines prefer around the number of 150 characters, but I recommend staying below that number to play it safe.

2. 404 Pages

404 pages are a royal pain, but they're quite easy to fix once you've identified them. Anytime you're linking to a page or image that doesn't exist, you're creating 404's for your users. Visitors are like deer and are very sensitive to slight movement. If they don't get what they want, they'll most likely leave to find it elsewhere.

You'd be wise to identify what's causing the 404 errors you have on your site and stop pointing to them. A tip that you can really benefit from is creating your own custom 404 page that is designed for the user. The best 404 pages out there display navigation, admit that there was a mistake, and have some humor on the page.

Google Webmasters Tools and the new Moz analytics are great tools to identify 404 errors.

3. Redirects

Google and other search engines prefer the 301 redirect over any of the following types:

- 302
- 303
- 307 redirects
- HTTP header refreshes

You'll be wise to apply a 301 redirect whenever possible. This will allow the link juice to follow its destined path (the others don't pass link juice). Here are some other things you should know about redirects:

- Google frowns on redirect hops past the number of about four or five. Play it safe by having no more than one or two.
- Only use a 301 redirect if you'll never send someone back to the original page!
- If you're unsure, you can use a 302 or a temporary redirect.
- Make sure you're using the 301 from the old page location to the new page location on the new site, rather than the new root domain.

4. Your Title Tag Is Too Long

You would think that this wouldn't be a problem, but it happens often. Search engines generally want lower than 70 characters. Now that everything is becoming more and more mobile, that number will probably shrink in the near future. We've got to get better at getting our point across with fewer words.

If this is a problem of yours, download a free SEO plugin in your WordPress dashboard and watch the number as you're typing it in. Stay below 70 characters.

Conclusion

Make sure you're staying on top of your SEO errors, notices, and warnings. The most common ones I see are title tags being too long, redirect issues, 404 errors, and missing description tags. You should make sure to fix these issues as soon as you see them coming in—a pile of these saved for later will add up and surely take a long time to fix.

What does WordPress SEO mean? I have been working doing PPC and SEO for the past couple years and I get asked questions daily concerning SEO. Beginners to the online world get confused about good SEO. Simply writing articles and sharing them on social media to drive traffic can't enable a site to rank well in Google. The quality of the article attracts only readers and subscribers through social media promotion. But, without receiving search traffic a site really won't go anywhere. Here's a short guide to WordPress SEO.

Chapter 13:

WordPress SEO For Beginners

This guide will help you to scale basic SEO for your site. The main aim of the SEO is to rank your website well in Google and to drive organic traffic to a site. To accomplish good SEO, you must consider a number of things about your site. Check out the list below to make sure your site ranks well in the SERPs:

1. Choosing the right keyword with Google's keyword tool will help you to attract the right customers. This isn't only for PPC people but for SEO as well.

2. Keyword placement is important to make SEO more appropriate for your website.

3. Build quality backlinks to your site. Quality is the key here— you need good links from reputable sites. If you don't' have links from reputable sites there is no need to get links at all. Focus on quality rather than quantity.

4. Make sure all articles are relevant and on topic to what you're trying to rank for with your WordPress site.

5. Add Alternative tags to every image you attach to an article and don't forget to add targeted keyword in the Alternative tag if possible, but don't go overboard. This isn't the most important but still, important. I always like to name images and I personally think that every little bit helps—Google is paying attention to everything. Again, don't go overboard.

6. Check for broken links both on your site and that point to your site. Broken links form a wall that will stop Google bots

from indexing the site and pages within your site. There's a simple WordPress plugin called Broken Link Checker you can use.

7. Avoid redirects on your blog if at all possible.

8. Have a valid XML sitemap. My favorite sitemap plugin for WordPress is Google XML Sitemaps Generator.

9. Use the keywords you're trying to rank for in the post. Make it natural though—it's not the percentage that matters, it's the content.

10. Stop reading articles about Blackhat SEO—Google hates it and will do anything and everything to stop it. If it's working now, it's only a matter of time before they kill it.

11. Consider catchy titles with targeted keywords presented in it. Catchy titles will attract readers' attention and spark their interest. Check out Topical Brainstorm to help you generate post ideas.

12. Avoid spelling and grammar mistakes.

13. Make sure to give each page a different description.

14. Maintain post frequency. Google loves sites with lots of high quality, fresh content.

15. Check out your competitors' links. These links will be key to your ranking for all the terms they rank for and more.

16. Link anchor text should target keywords you're trying to rank for. If you're trying to rank for "blue widget" then make

sure that you put that on your site or in a couple of your articles. Just don't go too overboard on this.

17. Outbound and inbound links are important aspects of SEO. Every post should include outbound links. Don't hoard links—link to useful things and people will link back to you.

18. When leaving a comment on another site, try and always enter in your website URL. This will drive traffic to your site. There really are no SEO reasons, but it's still a pretty good practice.

19. Choose the right keyword to rank better. It's always best to choose a keyword with low competition as to up your chances of gaining top rankings.

20. Choose keywords with minimum of $1 CPC—these keywords are easier to rank for.

Split Testing

It may sound kind of weird, but I've done experiments on how high or low a woman's shirt is in relation to the ad experience it receives. In the categories of no cleavage, a tiny bit of cleavage, and cleavage, I've found that a tiny bit of cleavage converts much better than cleavage. I found this all by split testing.

Many marketers, ourselves included, love to split test via A/B testing—this is when you test two or more different situations. When you're doing so, you can only split test one element at a time and must run the variations simultaneously.

Make sure you're A/B testing everything. Google likes better user experiences, so the goal is to find the ad text and landing page variations that resonate with the greatest amount of users. If you're giving your clickers a better user experience, you're going to find Google is giving you much better Quality Scores.

We'd like to share an example from a client of ours, ZacJohnson.com. He recently came out with a book on Amazon called "Confessions of a Six-Figure Blogger." We wanted to push people to a landing page to collect subscriptions and drive sales of his book, so we put up a landing page and started driving traffic. A couple days later we changed up that landing page to test something new and then a combination of the two.

Which one converted better? See the results below.

The first landing page was very bland with nothing really going on. The page converted at 2.5% on the back end, not all that bad. We drove 1,000 clicks to it to give it a really good shot. The total cost for this was around $1500.

The second landing page that we tested had big huge arrows (that no one could really ignore) pointing to where we wanted them to go.

What were our results?

The page had a 2.9% CTR. Our total cost was around the same amount through AdWords. This is positive outcome in our opinion.

Most people would stop here. They would take this page and then juice that page for everything its worth. Not us, we kept testing. We decided to add flashing arrows that pointed to the desired outcome. We then drove 1,000 clicks to that. Our CTR was the same as the others, as we weren't testing the ad copy but just the landing pages.

We had an increase in conversions on the back end of around 5.8%. Total cost was the same but our campaign doubled in profitability. Make sure you're always testing! We are currently still testing this landing page but haven't been able to get better than the current landing page.

Here are some well-known split testing tools:

- LinkTrackr
- Optimizly

Split testing is a technique used to experiment with live sites in order to find texts and headings that are highly useful and effective. I have used these countless times on my website http://blogging.org. We will use WordPress and compare it with the Website Optimizer used by Google to test different headlines in order to find out which functions best at capturing the Emails of clients.

Deciding on Your Experiment Type

There are two types of **testing—A/B testing** and Multivariate Testing. You have to choose one.

A/B Testing is used to test two dissimilar types of copy in order to find out the one that runs and converts best. Multivariate testing is best for testing many things at once. In fact, established online stores employ multivariate testing to find out which ad copies and layouts work best. In this case, we will use A/B testing.

Designing Experiment Flow

After deciding on the kind of page to use, the user first starts with signing up for a free eBook. After confirming subscription through Emails, the user is then taken to the goal page. Here, change things one after the other. If, for instance, it's the title page to be changed, the rest have to be maintained.

The Test Page Designing

To set up another page, first, log into WordPress, then, copy the information to your first page but under a different heading, then click "publish." This will enable the experiment to be set up in the Website Optimizer used by Google.

Designing the Goal Page

This comes after obtaining the access to the eBook.

Installing the Optimizer Plug-in

Installation of the code is facilitated by the Website Optimizer Plug-in. The code acts as a password to the goals page. To log in to the admin console, WordPress 2.8+ is used, then, click the plug-in and "Add New" at the bottom of the same page.

Setting Up the Optimizer Experiment

Log in to Google's website Optimizer through your Google account. You will be presented with two test options—A/B Testing and Multivariate Testing.

A/B Testing vs. Multivariate testing

Obviously, the A/B Experiment is our choice. To find out the effectiveness of the headings, click A/B and continue. At the page bottom, click "& create," to continue. After this, pick a name for the experiment; identify the pages to be tested and last the conversion page.

The Optimizer Code Installation

With the code provided by Google, access the control panel of your WordPress and go to the initial page you created. Then, enable the Website Optimizer. After that, insert the Control Script (first) and Tracking Script (second) codes provided by Google. Save the page, and proceed to the second page. At this point, use only Tracking Script (second).

Then, access and insert the Conversion script in the "Goal" page. Finally, publish the page. This is running the A/B Test. In the end, Google will let you know which page was the winner.

Chapter 14:

Hosting

Electricity is to house as hosting is to websites. Every house needs electricity and every website needs to be hosted.

Not all hosting companies are created equal—some are rather slow and others are quite reputable. Some are free and others cost money. When determining a hosting company to go with, decide what it is that you need and plan accordingly.

To see a list of the top 25 hosting companies, visit this link: http://blogging.org/blog/top-25-hosting-companies/

To see a list of the top 25 free hosting companies, visit this link: http://blogging.org/blog/top-25-free-hosting-companies/

Everybody looks for something different in a hosting company. It's something that every business in the world needs, but most don't know where to find. In this section I'm going to analyze some of the top hosting companies in the world and what their founders claim to be the most important factors when choosing a hosting company. Here are a few of the companies I'll be reviewing:

- **HostGator**—Customer service
- **Net Hosting**—Dedicated server hosting provider & security
- **Rackspace**—Public cloud solutions
- **SingleHop**—Server automation
- **Amazon**—Cheap without all the fluff

Customer Service

HostGator has received a number of awards for their customer service. In their press releases we learn from Support Team Lead Josh Banks that, "These awards acknowledge and affirm that we are absolutely doing the appropriate moves and going in the right strategic direction, especially pertaining to the depth and breadth of our commitment to ensure the highest standard of technical support."

Surprisingly, 90 percent of HostGator customers are fully satisfied with the quality of service they are getting. After each encounter with a customer, the representatives encourage the customers to fill out a survey.

Dedicated Server Hosting Provider & Security

After the GoDaddy hack, many business owners became increasingly more cautious of who they pick as a hosting provider. Many of those customers moved over to Net Hosting. Net Hosting founder Lane Livingston said, "I found that our unique value to the customer is not only our secure systems but the integrity of our company. Our customers can see that we truly care about them and want them to succeed online." In case you're wondering, they have six levels of 24/7 security, as well as state of the art Liebert UPS Systems.

Public Cloud Solutions

Drew Hendricks, who blogs for The Huffington Post said it clear, "Cloud computing is booming!" Storing information and hosting your business on the cloud is quite trendy. Reasons include, it saves time and money, it's easier, makes organization quite easy, and it's safe.

Rackspace considers themselves an "open cloud company." Lanham Napier, Rackspace's CEO, said, "we have had interest from service providers on nearly every continent to extend Rackspace's proven OpenStack-powered public cloud solutions and expertise to their customers. It is important to broaden the adoption of open-source technologies through partners around the world."

Additionally, the company stated, "Rackspace is passionate about leading this charge and helping service providers capitalize on the expanded network to better serve their customers."

Server Automation

When I was analyzing Singlehop, I was amazed at how tech savvy they were . Zack Boca said, "We empower you with the ability to control your infrastructure from anywhere, even on mobile devices. When you need more, you have more. Server automation is where technology is headed."

Cheap Without All The Fluff

If you host with Amazon, you could very well slash your hosting fees by half. Amazon's CTO, Werner Vogels, calls this "blogging like a hacker." Anytime you start trying to save a buck, you want to make sure you're comparing apples to apples. Just because it's cheaper may not necessarily be what you're looking for. Overall, if you're looking to host a static HTML site, Amazon hosting is the way to go.

When starting a business or trying to attract new customers to an existing business, PPC advertising can be a great tool. PPC campaigns are based on websites placing ad links to a business' website or specific product page in exchange for financial compensation when visitors click on the ad links. Ideally, webpages that PPC ads are placed upon share the same target audience as the business the ads are promoting, which makes an ideal working advertising relationship for both parties involved.

However, businesses planning on using the PPC method of advertising need reliable web hosting, whether through dedicated servers or alternative means. If a business' webpage lacks adequate hosting, all the money that is spent on PPC marketing may be a total waste.

Unreliable Webpages Don't Attract Customers

Once a site user clicks on a business' PPC ad, the business is obligated to pay the webpage the ad was placed upon for the click. If the webpage that the customer is directed to is experiencing an outage or not loading properly, odds are that the user will close the page and never think to return to it again. Therefore, all the ad has done is told a potential consumer that the company in question is unreliable and doesn't feel the need to invest in a reliable hosting option like <u>dedicated servers</u>.

Badly Hosted Webpages Lose Money

Every time someone clicks on a PPC ad link, a business has to pay the webpage promoting that ad, whether their webpage is working when someone clicks on it or not. Sure, the amount paid out for one click doesn't seem like much, but if lots of users are consistently clicking on an ad link that directs them to a webpage that is down, it is going to add up very quickly. This is one of the ways companies can directly and quickly lose money on otherwise promising PPC ad campaigns.

Consumers Don't Trust Webpages with Spotty Service

If a customer goes to input their credit card or PayPal information on a business' checkout page and the page fails to load or goes down, they might be forced to consider that the website they are about to put important financial information into isn't reliable. This may cause them to <u>reconsider their purchase</u> and not spend money on the website after all. Some consumers might even do more than decide against buying a company's product; they might even tell their friends that they think that the company is unreliable as well!

Can You Benefit from Free Web Hosting?

Not everything in life that is free has to be low quality. When it comes to creating a web site or blog you actually have a lot of paid and free web hosting services.

Free hosting doesn't mean you should stay away from them. Actually, it means you may want to investigate. Before deciding on a hosting service, make sure to document your website requirements. You don't know what hosting services you need until you know what your website needs to do. For example, do you need to sell products, allow for customers to review products and services, allow customers to submit documents, or are you just writing? Once you've written down your website requirements, you can investigate free hosting and paid hosting services. Blogging.org just released a list of the top 25 free hosting companies online, and you can view a full list here.

To save you some time, you can see a short list of the top five free hosting companies below.

1. *wix.com*
2. *weebly.com*
3. *000webhost.com*
4. *yola.com*
5. *edublogs.com*

Staying Up To Date With The Industry

Benjamin Franklin once said, "If I had four hours to chop down a tree, then I would spend three hours sharpening the axe and one hour doing the actual chopping." What was he trying to communicate here? It's better to swing at a tree with a sharp axe than a dull one. You could eventually knock the tree down with the dull axe, but it will take much longer.

Internet marketers need to sharpen their axe daily. They need to stay up to date with the industry and be on the cutting edge of technology. There are several ways to accomplish this:

- Subscribe to the RSS feeds of the industry leaders and experts—they will often release new and pertinent information.
- Attend industry events—associate and build relationships with others in the field.
- Read books published by industry leaders.

What companies should you follow?

- Google
- Yahoo!
- Apple
- Microsoft
- Facebook
- Moz
- SEJ

What leaders should you follow?

- Danny Sullivan
- Matt Cutts
- Rand Fishkin

Do you need help?

Both Murray and John do consulting to help businesses with their online marketing

Murray Newlands
@murraynewlands
http://www.linkedin.com/in/murraynewlands

John Rampton
@johnrampton
http://www.linkedin.com/in/johnrampton

Read more by us:

Murray
www.murraynewlands.com
www.themail.com
Online Marketing: A User's Manual.

John Rampton
http://www.huffingtonpost.com/john-rampton/
http://www.searchenginejournal.com/author/john-rampton/

Give us feedback

We would love your feedback to make this a better book for others. We do plan to update the book, what else would you like to see in it?

Printed in Poland
by Amazon Fulfillment
Poland Sp. z o.o., Wrocław